I hate y
talk to y
boy?

Guide For Parents Raising Their Teenage Son.

Catherine White

Table Of Contents

Introduction 1

Chapter 1: Parenting a Teenage Boy 2

Chapter 2: Power and Responsibility 12

Chapter 3: Turning Problem Behaviors and Respect 18

Chapter 4: Changes in Your Son and Psychology ... 33

Chapter 5: Connect and Communicate Effectively. 47

Chapter 6: What to Do and Not Do When Parenting Boys 56

Chapter 7: Getting Communication Right 67

Chapter 8: Establishing Teenage Rights, Privileges And Responsibilities 73

Chapter 9: Managing Fear and Risk 80

Chapter 10: Security and Lies 89

Chapter 11: Friends and Social Life 113

Chapter 12: Everything Parenting 129

Conclusion 136

Introduction

I want to thank you and congratulate you for downloading this book. You are making the right steps to learning more about your son, the changes that are happening inside of him during the next few years, and working to help create a health relationship for you and him as you both try to navigate this difficult road.

This book contains a wide variety of information to help you combat moodiness with your son and help you to navigate through these difficult and formidable years.

Let's Get Started!

Chapter 1: Parenting a Teenage Boy

Being a teenager's parent can be tough at times, and parents tend to question their parenting skills. In a bid to be a good parent, parents resort to over parenting. You must understand that being a parent is perhaps the hardest responsibility there is. However, indulging in over parenting does more harm than good. In this section, you will learn about certain signs that suggest that you are over parenting your child. Once you can recognize these signs, you can take corrective action. Apart from this, you will also learn about the common behaviors exhibited by a teenager.

Over parenting Behavior

It is perfectly all right to try and help your children. However, trying to micromanage their lives is referred to as over parenting. Regardless of how good your intentions are, over parenting isn't good. If you constantly hover over your son to ensure that he makes the right choices and try to shield him from the slightest of discomforts, it is a sign of over parenting. Another sign of overprotective behavior is to protect him from fully facing the consequences of his actions. Over parenting is usually the result of a parent's intention to manage their discomfort from seeing their kids stumble and fall. Or it could be because a parent is trying to overcompensate for any guilt the parent feels while disciplining their children. Here are a couple of signs that you are over parenting your son.

Frequent power struggles

Getting into constant power struggles with your kids is a sign of over parenting. For instance, it is okay to force your toddler to eat his vegetables to ensure that he stays healthy. However, if you get into constant power struggles with your teenage son about the way he dresses, styles his hair, or the friends he has is a sign of over parenting. You might have his best intentions at heart, but these things prevent him from finding the independence he is seeking.

Worrying about silly issues

It is okay to be concerned about the safety of your child. However, if you happen to be the only parent who is constantly worried about their teenage son going to school by himself or leaving him alone at home, it isn't right. It might be rather tempting to think that other parents aren't concerned. If you take a moment and think about it, it merely points out that you are over-concerned. If you don't start treating your son like an adult during his teenage years, how will he start acting like one?

Inability to witness their child's failure

No parent likes to see their kids stumble and fall. However, the best way to learn is through experience. If you come to your kid's rescue whenever he faces a slight inconvenience or do not allow him to solve his problems on his own, you are preventing him from learning. If you readily solve all your child's problems, he will never develop the ability to solve any problems he faces in life. Do you remember how your kid used to stumble and fall while learning to walk? Well, in the end, he did learn to walk, didn't he? Keep this in mind and trust that your child will learn.

Prevent the child from making his choices

Usually, parents seem to think that there is a right way to do certain things. However, this kind of thinking enables the parent to micromanage their child's choices. This goes back to the previous point once again. During teenage years, kids seek independence. To be independent, they need to make their own choices. If you force your choices onto him or prevent him from making his own choices, he will only end up resenting you.

Argue with other parents

Another sign of over parenting is getting into constant arguments with other caregivers in your son's life like teachers, other adults, or coaches. For instance, there might have been instances wherein you called up your son's school and demanded that his grade be improved, even when you know he didn't deserve it. Don't try to exert control over how others treat your son. Stop shielding him from the realities of life.

Improper expectations

Having high or extremely low expectations can also be a reason for over parenting. A lot of parents seem to enroll their kids in multiple activities. They do this to the extent that the child has no free time left. From your perspective, it might seem like a good idea since your child is always doing something productive. However, the reality is that you are trying to micromanage the way your child spends his time.

On the other hand, if a parent has extremely low expectations for their child, even that gives rise to over parenting. For instance, you might think that your child cannot do certain things and that you don't even give him a chance to get the work done. You might end up doing his projects or homework for him because you think your child cannot do it. Doing this takes away your child's individuality.

Division of responsibilities

Regardless of the expectations you have about your child, over parenting results in indulging your child. What is the difference between an adult working a job to feed their family and a 5-year old playing in the sandpit? The adult has responsibilities, whereas the toddler doesn't. Likewise, if you want your child to become a responsible adult, you must start giving him age-appropriate responsibilities. Over parenting can result in coddling your son and this will not prepare him for the challenges of the real world.

Over parenting might make you feel safe and relieve your anxiety about your child's wellbeing; however, it does more harm than good. Don't think that you are a bad parent. Since your intentions are good, you merely need to change your parenting style.

Common Behavior during Teens and Tweens

As the mom of two sons, I know that raising kids isn't always easy. As the child grows older, it becomes difficult. Adolescence is the transitioning time in any child's life from their carefree childhood to the responsibilities of adulthood. This is the phase in a child's life where he will try to portray his maturity and independence. He will face certain obstacles and failures too. All these things are a part of the learning experience but might frustrate him easily. As a parent, I know how difficult it can be to understand a teenager's behavior. However, there are certain things that almost all adolescents go through as they discover themselves. In this section, you will learn about the common behaviors you can expect from your child as he enters and goes through his adolescence.

Lashing out

You might notice a spike in the incidents where the child is yelling, screaming, or shouting. Also, it might seem like he is lashing out and getting into hurtful arguments. Well, verbal aggression is rather common. Usually, all the hormonal changes he is experiencing when combined with his want for independence results in verbal aggression.

Impulsive behavior

All the hormonal changes and the confusion brought about by teenage years can reduce your son's tolerance levels. Not just this, but his impulse control will be quite low too. A combination of different external factors like peer pressure, bullying, the lack of support at home, economic status, and such only worsens it. So, emotional outbursts are quite common. The next time your son has an emotional outburst, don't shout or yell at him. Instead, try to understand what he is trying to say. Children are impulsive. As the child steps into adolescence, he might be able to think like an adult but doesn't have an adult's impulse control. A combination of these factors means that he will make a lot of poor choices. Low levels of impulse control, when combined with peer pressure, means he will start taking risks. The desire to fit in with others is quite high during adolescence. He might not think things through before acting on his impulses. As a parent, it is your responsibility to correct him when things go wrong and help him get back up on his feet.

Spending more time with peers

A teenager will slowly start to withdraw himself from his family. He would naturally want to spend more time with his peers and don't be offended when your child does the same. It is normal and healthy. However, if you notice that your child is consistently withdrawing from all social interactions, it is time for an intervention. Adolescence brings about a lot of physical changes. Experiencing growth spurts means the teen will start to sleep longer and harder during those times. So, don't be surprised if your teen doesn't want to wake up in the morning or sleeps through the day on weekends. Apart from this, you will also notice that his appetite has increased noticeably. He might want several snacks between his meals. So, stock up the pantry with healthy and wholesome snacks.

Self-conscious about appearance

Apart from this, you will also notice that your teen has become rather conscious about his physical appearance. He might refuse to wear any off-brand clothes and might want to look fashionable. Don't be alarmed by all this. It is quite natural and don't be surprised if he takes a while getting dressed in the morning.

Desire for independence

Your teen will start fighting for his independence. It means that he will try to defy you and push you to your limits. Defiance is quite common. It might certainly frustrate you, but it is a part of growing up. Apart from this, it is quite common for teens to abandon their commitments. He might be interested in playing a sport and after a couple of weeks or months; he might no longer be interested. Don't be surprised, and it is not a reason to panic. He is merely trying to understand what he likes and doesn't. However, you can be concerned if it seems like he isn't interested in anything.

Self-esteem issues

A lot of teens struggle with low levels of self-esteem. The awkward stage of growth and his need to belong are the reasons for this. Your teen neither feels like a kid nor an adult nor starts to wonder where he belongs. This can lead to issues with self-esteem. Apart from this, peer pressure can harm his self-esteem too. Regardless of what you want to believe, peer pressure exists and is an undeniable part of growth. Until he learns to rise above it, he needs to learn to manage the same.

Selfish behavior

It is a general belief that teens are selfish. It might feel like all he thinks about is himself, his needs, and his convenience. He might act thoughtlessly and might not even consider the effect his words have on others. All this happens because he is trying to understand himself as a person. Since he is trying so hard to find his place in the world, he will have little or no time to think about others.

Rebellion

Be prepared to encounter several curfew violations. Every teen goes through a rebellious phase where they challenge authority, especially their parent's authority. Teens don't have a good sense of time and often lose track of time when with their peer groups. Don't jump to the conclusion that he is getting into trouble if he misses a few curfews. Usually, the reason is that he merely lost track of time. However, you can certainly set certain limits like asking him to message his whereabouts every hour or two.

Sense of identity

As I have already mentioned, most teens try to get a sense of their identity during adolescence. So, don't be shocked if your kid goes through emo, goth, or any other phase at this time. He might start dressing differently and might indulge in activities he didn't like in the past. Apart from this, he might also struggle with understanding his gender identity or sexual orientation. As a parent, I urge you to talk to your kids about all these things.

Mood swings are common

All the hormonal changes, like changes in the levels of serotonin and dopamine, taking place in his body means that he will be susceptible to mood swings. Don't be surprised if he seems happy one moment and cranky the next. It is normal behavior, and unless the mood swings are rather extreme, it is not a reason to panic.

Want for privacy

His newfound want for independence means he will naturally start seeking more privacy. Respect your teen's privacy and don't go snooping around his room. It is time to start treating him like an adult. You like your privacy, don't you? Likewise, so does your teen. Don't hover over him constantly and give him the space he wants.

Well, now that you know what you can expect during the teenage years, it will become easier to tackle any issues that come up. I am not saying that you can allow your teen to behave the way he wants, especially when such behavior is unreasonable. Instead, I am suggesting that you try to understand him. Once you understand him and feel what he does, it becomes easier to deal with him. You will learn more about all this in the subsequent chapters.

Chapter 2: Power and Responsibility

Teenage boys feel powerless, which interestingly enough, goes hand in hand with them feeling invincible. The perception of control over their lives is one of the most important gifts a parent can give their son. While it's important to have firm boundaries in place for your budding young man, it's important to make sure they know that you are giving them the chance to control the finer parts of their lives.

Dangerous Habits

Dangerous behavior is a result of feeling invincible, coupled with feeling powerless. Young men engage in these types of behaviors as a type of rebellion, to seize the moment and do what 'they want to', and most of the time they don't even realize how dangerous a specific action really is.

Take pornography, for example. It's just a few harmless pictures, right? Wrong. Roughly 25% of all internet searches are pornographic in nature and studies show that continued exposure to pornography not only is addictive, but can result in your son viewing sex, women, and relationships in a corrupted empathic way. So something that started as a simple choice can very quickly spiral out of control to something your son may not know how to handle. Drinking and driving or drugs could be other examples of something your son was only going to 'do once' and it quickly spiraled out of control.

Empower Them

So how do you help them feel powerful, brave, and manly without cutting them off from everything? It might be a good idea to expose them to something else that can help feel these roles. Sports are a great outlet for young men; it allows them to be physical, may possibly be an outlet for some testosterone driven aggression, and can make them feel powerful simply by winning.

Is your son not really in to sports? That's okay! There are tons of other 'exciting' and 'daring' activities that he can be a part of! Try mountain climbing, backpacking, hunting, skate boarding, and mountain biking.

Parent to the child, not by social standards. Every parenting book, article, and actual person has a different opinion about 'the best way' to parent your child. Sure, it's great to get advice, but that doesn't mean that you have to follow it. Stay away from hard lines, like "Teenagers should be this way" or "I have to do XYZ with my son", because the fact is everyone is different, and as a parent you don't have to follow any rule that doesn't serve the betterment of your child.

Allow them to make their own decisions, and if the decision is safe and does not cause permanent damage to their life or the lives of others, let them deal with the consequences. Don't undermine them by continuously questioning whatever it was they decided on, and if they do well with their decision making and follow the rules, reward them. Help your son to realize that the more responsible he is, the more power and freedom he will gain. By being trust worthy, it gives him more trust with you, and that will help him to do the things he wants to do without always having to ask for permission.

Be a Man

Society today teaches young men a hyped up sense of masculinity. Men 'aren't supposed to experience emotions' or 'cry' or 'let anyone disrespect them'. We are teaching our young men that 'respect', or maintaining it leads to violence, and if you don't 'man up' then your masculinity is somehow in question.

These types of thoughts can lead our young men to feeling like an outcast for 'having these forbidden feelings', with fear and worry being feminized emotions. All of this unsureity can lead to suicidal thoughts and actions because they feel so alone and down It's this type of thinking that, often times, gives the wrong impression about how to react or handle situations and can lead to aggression.

The Power of Men

Moms are great and certainly important to the rearing of children. In fact, there are plenty of single mothers out there who raised their sons all on their own without the help of a male in the picture. However, this doesn't mean that the power of a male influence in the lives of your son should be overlooked.

The unfortunate realization is, there are a many families in the US that are not only the product of broken marriages, but simply lack a male influence in the house at all. It's natural for younger males, even among animals, to look to the older ones to learn. They watch how men react to situations, handle their anger, communicate with others, and they learn from this and try to put it in to effect in their lives. Male contact during the teenage years, for your son, is some of the most important contact that he'll have in his entire life.

Fathers

Sons look to their fathers for most things that they do; the clothes they wear, the way they treat their mothers (and women in general), their work ethic, and how they interact with other men. This example fathers set is almost like handing your son a 'How To' guide for going through life, and if the example was poor, it would only be logical to expect the outcome and actions of your son's behavior to be poor as well.

Being open, available, and stable helps foster that relationship for fathers and sons, and more importantly, models how fathers should act with their children as well. Make time to spend with your son, and focus on the positive things they he does instead of harping on the negatives.

Mentors

It's not that parents aren't important; of course they are, but a mentor isn't a parent. They can't ground you for your opinion on something or take your cell phone away. They spend time with you because they want to, not because they have to, and simply by spending that time a mentor might take them out of situations where your son can become involved with drugs or alcohol. In fact, the more men in your son's life that are positive role models modeling the ideals you think are important, the better chance your son will have at modeling so those sale sorts of values.

Mentors can help provide perspective without judging, and this can make them ideal candidates for your son to open up to about the things happening in his life. Just the presence of a mentor has shown in studies to lower the risk of adolescents using drugs, and promote a better academic life as well as increase the chances for your son to go on to finish high education and training.

You can find mentors just about anywhere. There are professional mentors through 'boys to men' type organizations, but feel free to look closer to home. Churches are great for finding mentors that model your own moral code, but Uncles and close friends might be an option as well. Make sure you screen whoever it is you are allowing spending time with your son, just making sure the relationship is healthy for both of them.

Chapter 3: Turning Problem Behaviors and Respect

You're not magicians and there's no "silver bullet." Your teenage son is an individual who is bound to have a few kinks. All the same, he's one-of-a-kind, so applying blanket strategies is probably not helpful.

More important is the relationship you're establishing and improving by following the advice outlined in this book. A relationship is rooted in what two people know and like about each other. It's finding the common ground that bonds people together.

Family relationships are something we can't change. What we can change is our attitude toward what those means. When dealing with teenage boys and problem behaviors which may arise, it's important to keep a few things in mind.

Don't be "disappointed".

No matter what kind of mischief and mayhem your teenage son gets up to, telling him you're "disappointed" is only going to make matters worse.

Especially if you're building a strong bond and a healthy relationship with your son, there's nothing more undermining than expressing disappointment in a behavior. Your teenage boy may have no idea what he's done wrong, or how his actions have disappointed you.

Launching into an expository rant about why you're disappointed isn't going to take the sting out, either. Telling a teenage boy that you're disappointed in him is about the same as saying he "sucks" in his mind (which, as you'll recall, is not yet fully formed).

Be as disappointed as you like. But don't share that information with your kid. Hearing that will only push him away and make him feel like a failure. Remember how much he needs your support and use a different strategy.

Ask questions.

Your kid knows you're not pleased. He knows he's stepped over a line. This could be anything from smoking a cigarette, so getting a speeding ticket, to being suspended from school.

You needn't compound the terror of your teen boy. He's been caught. He knows there's a storm brewing. What he will not expect from you is to be treated like an adult.

That means you're going to sit down with him and discuss the error of his ways, certainly. But you're not going to rant about why what he did was wrong. You're going to ask him all the right questions to get to the root cause of the behavior.

Ask questions like these:

"Did you have any idea that what you were doing was going to have consequences? Did you even think about those?"

It's an honest question. It provides your son with an opportunity to explain what was going through his adolescent mind at the moment he decided to do whatever it was he did.

"What happened right before you decided to (fill in the blank)?"

This is an important question. The response will reveal whether peer pressure and a need to be accepted by the group was in play, prior to the action taken. If you hear that in your kid's response, the right course of action is to talk about why belonging to a group is less important than doing the right thing – even if it costs you friends.

If you have anecdotes about your own teenage years to share, that's even better. What you learned from those anecdotes will demonstrate to him that he's not the first teenage boy to mess up. He comes from a long line of former adolescents who've been there (and survived).

Drugs and booze.

These are big ones, to be sure. Let's not pretend that we all weren't naughty teenagers once and let's not pretend we didn't sneak booze from the parental liquor cabinet, or send some schnook into the liquor store to buy it for us.

Because we did and you know it.

Talking to your teenage boy about substance abuse is an important moment in his life. It's a defining moment. Alcohol is a legal substance, but only for adults. Underage people are not to be near the stuff. They're still growing and dependencies which can ruin their lives can develop quickly.

Opioid drugs may be legal, but they're also highly addictive. Talking to your kid about what they can do is key. This epidemic has taken thousands of lives all over North America and you can help your teenage boy recognize the danger.

As for illegal drugs, well – they're illegal. Getting caught with drugs can mean a permanent blot on a young man's life. Explaining that to your son and ensuring he understands what that means is key.

Not playing the saint, or the authority from above is key to a discussion with your teenage son about drugs and booze, especially if he's been caught in an institutional setting, like school, or even by the police.

Making it clear to your teenage son that you care deeply for his wellbeing is first. After that, sharing stories about how you learned to put substances (illegal and otherwise) in their place tells him you're willing to talk to him about it honestly.

Pretending you're perfect will only irritate and alienate him. While avoiding placing yourself on the same footing as your son, you're being open enough to invite him into a crucial conversation. You're acknowledging that he's ready to have a very adult exchange and to show him a side of you he may not have been aware of before.

Sexual misconduct.

How you manage this is highly individual. Your worldview about sexuality will factor in. One of the most important things you can do, depending on the situation - (Is someone pregnant? Has your son been caught in a compromising position?) - is to impress upon him that sex is normal and that sexuality is inherent to human beings.

You should also be talking about respect for his body. In the same you would talk to a teenage girl about the sanctity of her sexuality, you should be talking to your teenage son about it.

Sexuality is a sacred part of being human which is extremely precious. Talk about mutual respect and responsibility. Ensure your son knows enough about how reproduction works and how to avoid STDs and STIs.

Resist the (no doubt) overwhelming temptation to chastise him, but don't congratulate him, either. You're not high-fiving your kid for breaching boundaries, sexual or otherwise. You're guiding him through the labyrinth of growing up and part of that is being honest and open about sex.

Turning problem behaviors in your teenage son is rooted in the bond you're building and the relationship that bond is founded on. The more you respect each other, the less problem behaviors you'll need to turn.

Respect is a very important thing to many people. You know yourself that when you speak to your elders, your boss and strangers that you show respect and courtesy in order to earn their respect.

Now, as a parent, you also seek some respect from your children but what makes you think that your child doesn't seek respect from you? When raising children in general, making sure that you have their respect is important, but what about you? Even though your son is still a young man, you should know that he still wants to be respected no matter how old he is and if you want to connect and communicate with your son, the key is respect.

People say that one of the most important things when it comes to communication to any relationship, whether it is romantic, friendship, or a parent-child relationship, is respect. When you really think about it, it makes sense. Having a serious conversation with your child isn't going to go well if you do not show that you respect and hear their opinions and arguments. Along with this, it is important that you show your child that respect goes both ways.

Slouching and Grunting

If you have ever sat down to have a serious conversation with your son and only received "the slouch," some grunts and blank stares, then you have probably felt the frustration that comes along with trying to communicate with a teenage boy.

So before we dive into any theories and techniques on earning the respect of your teenage son and him earning your respect, let's have a chat about communication and how we can do this effectively.

When teenagers are being lectured about something they do not want to hear, they often dismiss the conversation. The information goes "into one ear and out through the other." This is definitely a big problem. Obviously, when you are telling your son something, it is usually for a good reason—maybe for his own good or to help him get through something. But giving your advice may be hard if the conversation is just being wasted on a person who isn't even taking it all in.

Here are some good ways to catch the attention of your son when you need him to hear you.

The first thing we should talk about is the idea of lectures. You know yourself that lectures are often boring and embarrassing when they come from authority figures. If you've ever been in trouble for a silly thing you'll know what how it feels. Understanding that lectures are sometimes demeaning is a sure sign that you are making progress.

You have to comprehend that your son doesn't like lectures any more than you do. The difference is that you are an adult and you know how to take these lectures with a grain of salt, heading the words of those who are giving them. Your son, however, is not at that level of maturity yet.

It might be a good idea to ditch the lecture for something else a little shorter and less demeaning. For example, you should compose a short list and let him know that "these are the things you did wrong, here's what you should do next time." This will help in the long run—your child might actually listen to you a little more.

Something else that you can do is to give him food! Yes, it sounds a little odd, but giving your teenage son some food before a good talk is something that you should give a shot. If you are a man, or if you were married to one, you'd know that back in the day they had their fair share of big meals. I know from experience that boys can eat a lot when they are teenagers, as well. So trust me.

Food makes a lot of people happier, too. When you give your child some food, you'll find that their mood might lighten and your words may actually be heard. Next time you want to have a chat with your teenager, do it over his favorite meal. It might get you somewhere.

Don't get mad! As stated before, it may be difficult to control and anger that you might have towards the young man or toward what he has done, but it is important to make sure that you control your emotions. Even if you are not mad and you are upset or happy, you do not want to cry! Crying is a good way to let your child know just how hurt or affected you are by his actions, but it also may shut him out. So you do not want to do that.

If you get mad, it could start a fight and cause a lot of tension between you and him. This could mean trouble, too. You would be bringing yourself all the way back to square one, virtually deleting all of your progress. So, just be careful of what you do and how much emotion that you show when you are speaking to your son.

You should also show that you are on the same team as your child; you do not want to fight. When you show him that you trust him, you are respecting his opinions and ideas. Make sure that you listen to his whole story. This will allow you to really "hear him out" and all for good communication.

Earning His Trust and Respect

When trying to connect with a teenager, it is all about finding out ways to earn their respect and help reassure them that they can trust you. You want to make sure that they can come to you when they need help and they need to be aware of the fact that you are not going to yell or scream at them (no matter how much you may want to).

But how do you connect with your son this way? How do you let him know all of these things without bursting into a lecture about what he should do and how he should do it?

The first thing that you should do when sitting down with your child would be to talk to him as if you have not been in this situation. Some parents do this when they compare their past situations to their child's. Even though this may be good for some teenagers, not all kids are going to connect to that. As they get older, they want to become more independent; they want to be their own person. You might be just trying to help him, but really, you could be fueling an internal fire to be different.

So try to talk to him as if you have never been through this before—even if you have. Ask questions, but not prying questions. You should be making him feel like he is having a conversation with you, it's not an interrogation.

Something else that you could do is show him that you trust him, too. Building trust is a two-way street, so when he sees that you trust him, he will slowly begin to trust you. This could improve your relationship on so many different levels.

Show him that you trust him by going to him when you need help. Maybe you are really busy and you need him to help you do the dishes. You could also confide in your son, letting him in on a financial problem, while asking him to not spend so much money. Follow your conversations with "Don't say anything, though". This will help him understand that you are telling him something that you don't want the world to know; a secret of sorts. Slowly, he will begin to open up to you, as well.

Finally, you should let him learn from his mistakes. A lot of parents make a bad decision and try to keep bad things from happening. The problem is, though, teenagers are sometimes going to run right towards what you do not want them to do! We all know this from personal experiences, movies, and TV shows.

What you want to do instead is to let him go through the experience, as hard as it may be, and allow him to see that it could have been avoided. He may even come to you for advice the next time around. Do not let him do anything that could harm him or others around him; stop him when it comes to that, even if it makes you seem like the bad guy.

Giving him the chance to become independent

Another good way to help you earn the trust and respect of your teen, is to try teaching—and allowing—him to become independent. This can be done in many different ways, one including giving your child a higher curfew or even their own bank account.

This might seem a little crazy when you think about it at first but, depending on the responsibility that your teen shows, giving them a bank account and a monthly or weekly budget to control themselves can help them in many ways! Giving him a budget to restrict their spending will teach him discipline as well as teach him independence in terms of buying his own lunches, snacks, and knick-knacks.

Make sure that you teach your son responsibility, as well. Giving him a bank account does this as well, but you can also teach him responsibility by giving him chores and business to do around the house. This could include doing his own laundry, cleaning his room weekly, or even picking up a younger sibling from school or certain activities. You can also make sure that you set rules for doing home work on the weekdays and Sunday.

When I was growing up, the rule was that our homework was to be done first thing when we came home from school. This way, we had the rest of the night to do whatever we wanted. Explaining it this way might help reduce any fights or disagreements that you may have with your children.

After so long of doing this, your son will understand why it is so important for him to do his homework right away and eventually you will not have to ask! When he gets older, he will no doubt be more independent in doing certain tasks later on in his academic or working life; he will be more responsible in general.

Doing other tasks around the home will also help build your child's responsibility and give him the chance to become more independent.

Independence can be taught by parents through accountability. When your son does something wrong, make sure that he knows that he is the only one that can fix the problem and he has to deal with the consequences. If your child does something wrong, do not lecture him, as we said before. Let him know what he did wrong and tell him what the consequences are. Tell him what he has to do to fix the problem that he has created.

For example, if you have smaller kids, you probably have toys made specifically for those younger children. If your teenager breaks it, you should tell him that he has to use his allowance or monthly budget to pay for a new one! That way he knows that what he did was wrong and he has a good idea of what is going to happen if he does it again.

This is a very simple example, however. Things can get worse when it comes to raising teenagers, but you just have to take it one step at a time. If your child is arrested, for example, for a minor crime—something that he can be fined for. Make him stay in jail for a night before you bail him (if need be) and then make him pay the ticket or work it off if you have to buy it.

All of these things put together should help your child understand the problems that come with misbehaving and help teach him credibility and responsibility, as well.

Allowing your child to experience any kind of labor is another way that you can assure that he is becoming more independent. Getting him to apply for summer jobs, volunteer work, or even odd jobs around the neighborhood will help a lot with many of the problems that we've talked about so far

When this young man begins to work and he knows that what he does wrong could deduct pay or get him fired, he will understand that his best behavior is most suitable for the workplace. This shows both credibility and responsibility! He will also learn independence and responsibility with his money, as well. The money that your son earns is all his to spend. Hopefully, if you get him a bank account, he would already know just how to spend his money wisely.

Discipline is also an advantage to introducing your teenager to the working world. Showing up on time and following orders and instruction are things that your child will have to get use to no matter who it is coming from. It may be frustrating to him at first and he might complain, but you just have to explain that a lot of people don't like their bosses and you just have to deal with it! Insert some humor in there to lighten the mood and make him smile.

Chapter 4: Changes in Your Son and Psychology

The transition from a child to a teenager can be tricky. The common cognitive, emotional, psychological changes that your son might undergo during his transition to becoming a teenager are discussed in this section.

Common Changes when Boys Transition into Teenagers

Adolescence can be a bumpy ride for not just the parents, but the kids too. However, you can reduce this turbulence. If you try to understand the changes your kid goes through and the challenges that you might have to face, you can work through all obstacles that come your way. One of the rather dramatic phases of development that your son will go through is adolescence. During this phase, he tends to become fully aware of the developmental process. Understand that your son can watch and experience the changes taking place and has to accept the same. Your child will undergo several physical, cognitive, social, and personality changes during his teenage years. Phew, that's a lot for anyone to take in! While he is undergoing these changes, he also needs to accept these new changes. Coming to terms with all this might not always be a pleasant experience for him. You can help him along the way if you are aware of the changes he will undergo. Here are certain changes that your boy might experience while transitioning into his teenage years.

While transitioning from tween to teenage years, your child undergoes a lot of changes. These changes are a rather big deal for him. Kids tend to face certain bumps during their teenage years. The level of physical maturation they undergo influences the extent of these bumps. For instance, social awkwardness can be caused if he matures earlier or later than his peers. Also, puberty tends to cause certain awkwardness in the relationship shared between a child and his parents.

Experiencing growth spurts, developing facial hair for the first time, significant hormonal changes not only affect the child but the parents too. On top of everything, the constant worry of having to measure up to the impossible ideal of the perfect physique propagated by social media further pressurizes the child. Believe it or not, your child is constantly worrying about being under or overweight, being too hairy, and so on.

Did you know that once your child hits their teenage years, different areas of his brain start to develop rapidly? As a result, by the time he is between 15 to 16 years old, he can use logic and reason the way an adult does. However, the portion of the brain, which is responsible for planning and thinking ahead needs a while to develop. This is primarily the reason why a lot of teens tend to make poor decisions, especially when it comes to taking risks, using alcohol, engaging in sexual activities, and any other risky behavior. Essentially, a part of his brain can think and act like an adult, whereas the other part cannot. Your son might be able to understand the logic behind why a certain thing is right or wrong, but his brain isn't fully mature enough to grasp the consequences of such actions. A teenager's brain undergoes certain cognitive developments, but it isn't fully matured yet. The changes that he undergoes can cause turbulence in a parent-son relationship.

A change, regardless of how desirable it is, isn't always easy. When a child enters his adolescence, he is trying to understand who he is. It is often referred to as an identity crisis. It isn't a bad thing, but it isn't always a comfortable transition. It might not sound like much to an adult, but during their teenage years, a child needs to make a lot of decisions. He needs to decide who he wants to be in life, what his morality is, his temperament, his sexuality, opinions about politics, and so on. Apart from this, he also needs to make career-related decisions. That's a lot to take in and can be a source of enormous stress. This process of self-discovery isn't easy and can cause tension in their personal relationships.

There are several social changes, but the most significant of all is when the child develops his independence. Some teens start exhibiting signs of independence earlier than others. However, almost all teens will start spending less time with their parents at this point. They start to feel quite comfortable and secure with their friends or their peers more than their families. Also, this is the time when they start forming rather complicated relationships. Sexual attraction and dating have become quite common. His hierarchy of preferences tends to change when it comes to relationships. Don't be surprised if your son seems to want to spend more time with his peers or partners. This change can also be another reason for conflict.

The two major challenges which you will face as a teenager changes are independence and communication. You must learn to deal with his push for independence and learn to communicate even when he seems unwilling to. It is not surprising to note that teenagers often want to do things earlier than what the parents deem as being appropriate. This applies to everything from the way he dresses, to owning a phone, following curfews, or even going out with his friends. Everything will become a negotiation where he will try to assert his sense of independence.

He might not wish to discuss his life with you, and don't be offended by this. It is a very common change that all teens go through. Most parents might find this rather disconcerting, but by learning to communicate with him, you can overcome this obstacle. As a parent, you might feel a little neglected or even rejected. You might start to think that your child no longer loves you or needs you. However, this is merely a face when he is trying to discover himself. You will learn more about communicating and connecting with your teenager in the subsequent chapters.

Psychology Involved

Understanding the psychology of the parents and your teenage son will give you a better idea about parenting. It will give you the insight necessary to understand your growing teen. In this section, you will learn about the psychology of the parents as well as their teenage boys.

Psychology of a Teenage Boy

It is often believed that teenage boys are full of angst. However, once you delve into the psyche of a teenage boy, you will realize that they experience a myriad of emotions. It is quintessential that you understand what he experiences if you want to learn to parent him. Teenage boys certainly bring about a lot of changes with them. Your kid is trying to come to terms with the fact that he is no longer a boy and is now headed toward becoming a man. Teens tend to give the impression that they are often frustrated, uncertain about themselves, and stressed out. However, you must consider the fact that they are undergoing major physical, emotional, and cognitive changes during their teenage years. This is a major overhaul for your teen too. Therefore, it is not surprising that they feel uncertain.

I often wonder what turned my once sweet and innocent child into an impulsive, risk-taking teenager. I am sure that even you wonder about this. Well, the answer to this lies in the allotment of the brain. The common traits that a teen exhibits like exasperating the adults, indulging in impulsive behavior, showing poor judgment, and social anxiety are all related to the teen's biology. Even stubbornness and rebellious attitude can be related to their changing biology.

You might clearly present certain arguments and lay down certain thoughts in front of your teen, which make perfect sense to you. However, it is not a good idea to assume that your teen perceives all of this the same way that you do. As mentioned, the brain undergoes a major overhaul during the teenage years. When this happens, the behavior and thought process of your teen changes too. For instance, a teenager might drive his car too fast around a curve and crash into a lamppost. He might have seen the speed limit signs, undergone the necessary tests to obtain his license, and heard all the driver's safety tips given to him by spirits. Even after all this, he somehow managed to act without thinking and crashed his car. Well, all this goes back to the way his brain is developing.

The white matter that is present in the brain's frontal cortex is responsible for all his poor judgments. Decision-making, the ability to decide, making judgments, and impulse control are all associated with the frontal cortex. The white matter microstructure relays the signals between the grey matter and the neurons. During the teenage years, white matter starts to form, and the unnecessary grey matter disappears. Well, all this sounds too complicated. Here is a simple example for you to get a better understanding of how your teen's brain works.

Think of all the neural pathways as electrical wiring. The bare or live wire is dangerous. It needs some degree of insulation. Insulation helps to protect the wires while improving its ability to relay signals. So, the more insulation there is, the better the signals will be relayed from one point to another. Since this insulation starts to form in the teenage years, it can be one of the reasons why a teenage boy behaves impulsively. Not everything can be blamed on biology, but denying this relationship is not a good idea.

Well, enough with the technical stuff. Let us look at some simple things that your teen keeps thinking about. Being a guy is certainly not an easy task. We all live in a society, which has conditioned us to believe that men have to be tough. Your son is trying to find his place in the world while trying to live up to this unrealistic expectation. This can be a source of immense stress for him. Apart from this, he needs to deal with peer pressure too.

All teens go through an awkward phase. Your son might be going through this phase at the moment. He might have started to experience certain things, physically as well as emotionally, which he hadn't in the past. This is a lot to take in. Often, it tends to overwhelm teens and make them feel uncertain about themselves.

Apart from this, he can be worried about rejection and might be insecure about himself. We all live in a world that's dominated by social media. From the time he wakes up in the morning until he goes to sleep at night, he is surrounded by social media. Social media is helpful, but it often propagates unrealistic expectations of how people should look or how they must live their lives. So, your teen might feel insecure that he doesn't belong in this oh-so-perfect life. Well, it can be rather tough.

He also has to come to terms with the reality of the way life works. He might have imagined that his life would unfold in a certain manner. This might not happen, and it can be a source of frustration for your teen. He is also trying quite hard to find his place in the world. The need to be accepted by his peers and finding his identity are quite real for your teen. Apart from this, they start becoming quite conscious about the way they look. The body starts to change, facial hair starts to grow, and all these things can certainly make him feel conscious. This is especially true if he is maturing at an age which is faster or slower than that of his peers.

Well, that's a lot of stress that your teen is facing. Understand that his brain hasn't fully accepted all of this yet. If he's acting out or lashing out, it is mainly because of his inability to come to terms with all of this. As a parent, you must understand that he is facing all of this. If you want to connect with him or want to form a close bond with him, then you must try to understand him. Try to recall your teenage years, the awkwardness you went through, or the uncertainty you felt. I'm sure you also experienced all these things. Then why is it surprising to know that your teen is undergoing the same? So, parents, take a step back and try to see the world from your teen's perspective.

Psychology of Parents of a Teenage Boy

All the changes that come along with adolescence are not just hard for the adolescent but for the parent too. Most of the tension can be reduced when the parent starts to understand why the child behaves the way he does. I've noticed that a lot of parents with young kids tend to be filled with a sense of dread when they realize that they have to deal with a teenager soon. Teenagers are risk-takers because they don't have a sense of judgment to understand the consequences of their actions or words. They will also try to push away from their parents or even family members. They prefer to be in the company of their peers and others their age. Teenagers can become rather difficult to communicate with and show signs of rebellion. Parents can start to feel that they're being rejected by their teenage kids, and this can be rather hard for the parent.

I remember all the times when I felt neglected, helpless, and even worried about how to treat this new person my son was becoming. I'm sure you might have experienced these emotions along with some infuriation or annoyance as well. Your child's refusal to follow your rules or spend time with you can make you miss the child that he was until a couple of years ago. These things might be true, but you need to understand that your child is growing up. Teenage years can be a wonderful time too if you change your perspective towards it. For instance, your teenage son could be full of energy, enthusiasm, and wide-eyed amazement at all the possibilities that the world has to offer. He will start showing signs of empathy that a toddler doesn't. During this time, he will start thinking like an adult. It means that you have a greater chance of connecting with your child at an adult-like level. Apart from all this, you can take a moment to appreciate the person your child is becoming.

When the tween years come to an end, your child enters teenage years, and after a couple of years, he comes out an adult. However, this progression from adolescence to adulthood can be turbulent. In this section, we'll learn about the different things that a parent feels, that you feel when your child enters his teenage years.

Direction in life

Parents tend to go through certain adjustments of their own too while their kids go through teenage years. They are also trying to come to terms with all the changes that the teen is going through and are trying to cope with it. At this stage, parents tend to realize the fragility of their age while their kid is still very young. A mother is almost at the end of her childbearing years, whereas her kid is just entering those years. You might realize those different avenues in life which were once open to you are no longer available. Whereas, new opportunities are opening up for your child. There is almost a sense of irony to all of this. It is normal for a parent to experience a sense of uncertainty or even envy. Don't think of yourself as a bad parent if you're jealous of all that your child has which you no longer do. It is merely a part of growing up. Yes, it is a phase of growth for the parent too.

Grappling with reality

From late-night feedings, to the time your son took his first steps, to the first day of school, to him becoming a man. This is a lot for a parent to take in. Coming to terms with the reality that your child is no longer the toddler that he once was is not an easy change. You need to come to terms with the reality of the person that your teenage son is becoming. You might have had an image of your extremely popular and extroverted child in your mind. However, in reality, your child is an introvert who likes to keep to himself. Or perhaps, you've had a vision that your son is an academic virtuoso, but he has an inclination towards arts and sports instead of academics. As a parent, you might experience feelings of disappointment or even frustration that your teenage boy is nothing like what you imagined in your head. Well, reality often differs from what we visualize it to be. It is essential that you come to terms with all these changes and accept your son for whom he truly is.

Style of discipline

You must set certain ground rules along with the consequences of breaking those rules. These rules must be non-negotiable. However, it is time that you take a different approach towards discipline and your teenage son. You might not feel that your child is ready for all the freedom available in the world. However, it is not for you to decide. You might feel scared that you can no longer protect your little one.

However, it is time to understand that he is no longer a child and is on his way to becoming a man. You cannot try to discipline an adult the way you would discipline a kid. For instance, as a tween, his curfew might have been 9 pm. Now, he is no longer a tween and is a teenager. So, it is time to renegotiate this rule. Don't try to be too fix upon certain ideas you have in your head about what he should and shouldn't be doing. Instead, treat him as an equal and talk to him about the changes that he would like. By doing this, you both can come up with a list of rules and regulations. Perhaps you can ask him to come up with the consequences of breaking those rules too. Doing this will make him feel like an adult and at the same time, make him realize the fact that abandoning responsibilities comes with consequences.

Time to let go

You cannot micromanage your child's life or schedule. It is time to realize that you need to let go. It is not an easy task for a parent to let go of their son. To be fair, you have been, or rather he's been an integral part of your life so far. I remember when my son started pulling away. I too felt a little sad that he no longer needed me. Well, understand that he is just carving out independence. It doesn't mean that he stops needing you. It just means that he's exploring his life. Give him the freedom to explore his life and shape his reality for himself. The harder you try to hold onto him, the more resistance he will put up.

Staying connected

I know it feels like your child is pulling away from you. It does become a little tricky to stay connected with your teenager. However, there are ways in which you can do this. Don't be disheartened if he doesn't want to spend as much time with you as he did in the past. Instead of feeling bad, you can come up with different ways in which you can stay connected with him.

Acknowledging his sexuality

As your teen is coming to terms with his sexuality, it is time for you to embrace the same. You need to find ways in which you can accept and also deal with the sexual choices your teen makes. If your child feels like you don't support him, he will withdraw. Instead, show him that you love him unconditionally, regardless of his sexual orientation.

Chapter 5: Connect and Communicate Effectively

Effective and efficient communication is essential to maintain a healthy relationship. In this section, you will learn about how you can connect and communicate with your teenage son.

Steps to Connect with a Teenage Son

As my son started inching towards adolescence, I became abundantly aware of how our relationship was changing. I realized that he was no longer interested in following me around like he used to. It was surprising that he didn't want to share as many details about his life as he used to. I still remember when he came home after his first day of elementary school and was excited to talk about all the new things he had experienced. While, when he started high school, I noticed that he was withdrawing himself more. If I could manage to get a complete sentence from him insofar as a shrug or a grunt as a response, I started to feel lucky. I was tired of hearing "I don't know," and "whatever" as responses.

I started to miss all the times that we spent reading books together and cuddling when he was a little boy. I knew that he needed his space and that for him to grow up he required independence. However, the mother in me could not accept that I was unable to connect with my son. It is quite difficult when he starts to pull away. A lot of parents simply give up because they don't know what to do. Let me tell you a little secret, you can always connect with your son regardless of his age. In this section, you will learn about certain things you can do to stay connected with your son.

Understand him

Try to get to know him and understand what really matters to him. You can ask him questions but don't be nosy and don't try to pry. A simple question that you can ask your son is, "What is bothering you?" I am sure that he will open up if not immediately, then eventually. Ask him how school is going on and about his friends. Try to get to know his friends. Learn about the kind of music he likes or the food he relishes. Try to be open and curious about the things he likes. Once he notices that you are making an effort, he will reciprocate. Ask him about the things he likes and doesn't. If you don't agree with something that he likes, then instead of writing it off, try to see it from his perspective. If you are unable to do this, then ask him why he likes what he does. Try to get him to start talking and you will be able to find common ground.

A little special treatment

You can do something that is just for him and it will show that you love him. At times, a little reminder that you are there for him and that you love him is necessary. It can be something as simple as cooking something that he loves. This is all it takes to reconnect with your teenage son. Make his favorite meal, sit down with him, and talk to him. Try to be more involved in the kind of activities that he likes.

Validation matters

Understand that he is going through a challenging and crazy time in his life. He will need his space at times, so give it to him. It isn't just you who is facing challenges. Your teenage son is torn between desiring independence and needing you. Have faith, even if it looks like he's pulling away right now, he will come back. However, for this to happen you need to make a conscious effort. Be mindful of the way you talk to him.

Don't engage in any power struggles and let go of all petty arguments. Your son might say hurtful things in the heat of the moment but holding onto those words will only hurt you. If you have a problem, then wait for him to calm down, and then you can talk to him about it. Don't restrict his choices, and instead let him decide. He does see your approval and validation. If he seems genuinely excited about something and you don't clearly understand it, then try to understand it. Try to validate his feelings and don't make him feel like they don't matter.

Plan a fun activity

A simple way to connect with your teenage son is to do something fun together. It can be something as simple as sending him funny texts or memes. If you come across something that you think he will enjoy, share it with him. Make it a point to engage in some fun activities together. Maybe you can create a playlist together and watch a movie. Do something that you both enjoy, and it will give you a chance to bond. There are plenty of things you can do together!

Let him choose

Allow him to choose and give him a chance to be the expert. If you're struggling with the latest gizmo or need some technical help, then ask him. The feeling of being helpful to one's parents can be quite enriching for a child. Maybe you can both listen to a podcast or watch a video together. Even if it doesn't interest you, try to do something with him. It gives you a chance to talk about the things that he likes and get involved in his life.

Getting something done together

Maybe you can do something together. It can be something as simple as going out for a haircut together. Regardless of the haircut he chooses, don't react negatively to it. You're trying to reconnect with your child and strengthen the bond you have. So, it is important to allow him to understand that you are there for him. You can ask him for his help with grocery shopping or offer to do any other activity that you like. If he allows you to, then maybe you can help him organize his room. Don't start nagging, criticizing, or lecturing him while doing any of these things. If you don't agree with something, then ask him to explain it from his perspective. While he is doing this, ensure that you're carefully listening to him. The way your child thinks will certainly be quite different from the way you think.

Essentially, the idea is to spend as much time with him as you possibly can. All these ideas might not work for you, but something will; it's a process of trial and error. Keep trying different activities with different approaches until you find one that clicks.

Tips to Establish Efficient Communication

Communicating with a teenage boy might seem like an art at times. The good news is, you can learn to do this. In this section, you will learn about the different tips you can follow to establish effective communication with your teenage son.

There exists an undeniable connection between anger and hunger. So, a simple thing to do is make sure that neither of you is hungry before starting a serious conversation. Making sure that his sugar level is stable will prevent the chances of any grouchiness. Also, when he is well fed, his ability to engage in conversation and stay focused improves.

It is a good idea to notify him in advance about the topic as well as the time when you plan to talk to him. Don't expect him to go into the conversation with a list of points or counterpoints that he wants to make. However, it does give him some time to think about the things you want to talk about. It allows him to present his thoughts and ideas in a clear manner. Not just that, it also gives you some time to think about the things you want to talk about.

If you want to converse with your child, then forget about lecturing him. If you talk to him in a condescending tone or start lecturing him, then it will certainly put an end to a discussion. The chances of the discussion escalating into an argument are quite high when you start lecturing your child. Instead of lecturing him, it is a good idea to keep things brief. Just get to the point and talk to him about the topic at hand. Also, the chances of miscommunication increase when you start beating around the bush instead of getting to the point.

Apart from this, it also increases the chances of your son zoning out while you're talking. You must learn to manage your emotions. Don't allow them to get the best of you. Your son might say or do things to trigger you, but don't give in to the urge to react. Instead, learn to respond carefully. You can diffuse even the tensest of situations by responding calmly. You cannot control the way your son thinks or behaves. However, you can control the way you respond to all these things.

Boys tend to think better when they are active or are engaged in some sort of movement. So, you can start talking while walking or doing something else. If you force him to sit down and then engage in a conversation, it just makes the whole thing seem rather forced and formal. Instead of doing all this, it is a good idea to go on a walk with your son and then talk to him about something. Also, the chances of reacting violently tend to decrease when you are engaged in a physical movement.

At times, it is better to communicate indirectly. If you constantly stare down your son while having a rather important conversation, then it can make him feel threatened or suggest aggressive behavior on your part. You don't want to come across as being aggressive while having an important discussion. So, I suggest that you have certain conversations while walking side-by-side or even while driving. The best way to have an important discussion is to only occasionally make eye contact. This will make your son feel calm and relaxed. The more relaxed he is, the more open he will be about communicating.

You can guide him and tell him when he does wrong. However, stop yourself from patronizing him. If he feels like he doesn't have any power, then it will merely trigger his fight or flight response. The feeling of helplessness can effectively end the conversation.

For instance, instead of telling him what he needs to do, you can ask him what you can do to help him. Or perhaps you can ask him what his plan of action is to accomplish what he wants. Also, never assume anything while talking to your son. When you assume things, it not only increases the chances of miscommunication, but also puts him on the spot. For instance, you can ask him if he's dating anyone instead of asking him whether or not he has a girlfriend. By keeping things general, you make it easier for him to open up to you.

It is not just about talking but it's also about being a good listener. If your son feels like you're not listening to him, then he will immediately clamp up. This is something you want to avoid. So, don't interrupt him while he's talking and actively listen to him. Ask follow-up questions to show that you have been listening to him. When he feels like he's heard he will want to talk to you more often. Instead of judging or telling him that he's wrong, ask him what he feels. Take a moment to listen to him and carefully analyze what he's told you, and then think of a positive way in which you can respond. We all like to be heard and the same stands true for your son too. So, be a good listener.

It might not always be easy to understand what he says. At times, you might even be against his ideas or thoughts. However, try to see things from his perspective. Instead of putting him down, ask him to explain things to you. Show him that you are curious about what he thinks and that you're willing to understand his perspective. Doing this is not only respectful towards him but will encourage him to talk to you more. Also, it increases the chances of him responding in a respectful and pleasant manner. Try to keep a neutral perspective on the topic at hand. Don't formulate opinions or jump to any conclusions. Wait for your son to finish his piece and then talk to him about it.

People say things when they are hurt, angry, or frustrated. Give your son a little leeway. If you are hurt by something he has said or done, then talk to him about it once he has calmed down. Keep reminding him that you are there for him and that you will support him. If he sees encouragement and unconditional support, then he will want to be more involved with you. He needs to understand that he can depend on you, and that he isn't alone.

There will be certain topics that your child will not want to discuss with you. It is bound to happen and is natural. Don't force him to talk about something that he clearly doesn't want to share with you. When he is ready, he will share with you. However, for this to happen, you need to show that you love and support him. Only when he feels like you will keep an open mind, will he come and talk to you about it. Don't let it bother you, if he doesn't want to share something. Remember that when he is ready, he will come to you. Don't push to talk about something. If you do this, you are merely pushing him away. Perhaps, your teen is comfortable talking about this to someone else or maybe one of his peers. If that's the case, then let it be so.

By following these simple steps, you can ensure that you're able to communicate effectively and efficiently with your teenage son. So, the next time you're talking to him, make sure that you follow at least some of these steps. Do this for a while, and you will see a positive improvement in the relationship you share.

Chapter 6: What to Do and Not Do When Parenting Boys

How do you raise a boy? How do you help him grow up to be a loving, responsible and confident man?

Don't Be Overprotective

Part of a mother's nurturing ways is always to love and protect. But when nurturing turns to coddling and becomes excessively protective, you can cripple your son for life.

Part of your responsibility as a parent is to encourage your child to be independent. You can raise him to be a mama's boy (or a daddy's boy) and share an undeniable bond with him, but you have to be careful that you are able to let go when it is time to let him go and do things on his own.

So, when your son wants to play in the mud, let him, even if it means dirty hands and feet and more soiled clothes for you to wash. When it's time to start preschool, send him off even if you have to leave him crying with his teacher. Make him clean up his own messes instead of cleaning up after him all the time because he needs to learn that life is not always easy.

As your boy matures and goes into the world on his own, be excited for him despite your protectiveness.

Help Him Make Decisions on His Own

Part of preparing your son for adult life is teaching him to be self-reliant.

You can start even at a very young age by giving him opportunities wherein he can choose. One of the areas that children want to have a say in is in what he gets to wear.

I remember when my son was in preschool and I would lay out the clothes I would want him to be wearing. There were days he would say, "I don't want to wear that, Mommy!" And I would go, "Ok, baby, go pick out what you want to wear for school." He absolutely loved that we would go back and forth together as I helped him choose the right colors that go together. I think it even made him more eager to go to school. Of course there were days that he would choose to wear some silly outfit, like his Spiderman costume or his pajamas. So I would firmly tell him no, and with a pretty little pout he would ask why, and I would go on to explain why sometimes he can't just wear what he wants and that it's important to always dress up properly.

As much as you can, try to create situations where your child can choose and always guide him when he makes these decisions. Praise him when he makes the right ones and step in when he makes poor choices. Make it clear by putting it in plain words why you had to say no so that he can make better choices next time.

Don't Be Too Indulgent

It's natural instinct for any parent to want to give his child everything he wants. However, even if as parents we can afford to give him what he wants all the time, realistically we know that over-indulging will only lead to spoiling him. We don't want to raise a selfish and insensitive boy but a responsible and compassionate man.

The most sensible thing is to teach your boy to be responsible with his gifts. If he receives what he wants, teach him to be grateful and how he has a role of taking care of it. If money is hard up at times and he can't have what he wants, don't hesitate to point out that you can't afford it for him. This way, you make him aware of many valuable life lessons such as: 1) that not everything can be handed to him, 2) that he has to live within his means, and 3) that he shouldn't give too much importance on material things.

Teach Him How to Manage His Feelings

Boys typically have a much harder time than girls in communicating their emotions. As a parent, a big part of your responsibility is to teach your son that it's okay to feel – that feeling sad, angry or afraid is part of being human and that he needs to convey his feelings the right way so the he can be clearly understood.

Our society has stereotyped boys to be the strong, silent types and they grow up believing that they're not allowed to show emotions so openly. The tendency for most parents is to repress those emotions, "Don't cry, boys don't cry!" The sad fact is that these inhibitions don't help him learn how to deal with his feelings in the right way. They grow up not knowing how to communicate well and having a hard time relating to others.

As young as possible, get your son to talk to you so that he'll grow up feeling comfortable with it. When you notice he's feeling grumpy, for example, ask him why he's upset and invite him to talk about it if he wants to. Don't force it out of him, but issue an invitation like, "You can talk to mommy if you want, I'd love to help you."

Don't stop at talking. Help him focus on a solution instead of the problem. Dan Kindlon, PhD, an assistant lecturer at Harvard School of Public Health and coauthor of Raising Cain: Protecting the Emotional Life of Boys says that "boys prefer to focus on the problem rather than the emotion." Offer up some ideas that will enable him make things better.

Always give assurance. If you can't get your son to talk, give him a hug. That simple gesture can sometimes work more wonders than a thousand words can. Just let him know that it's ok to feel bad and that things will get better.

Don't Label Him

Never limit his creativity and spontaneity because of his gender. Part of your responsibility is to help him build a healthy sense of self-esteem. Allow him to explore his interests, even if he does so in the most unconventional ways just as long as he doesn't disrespect other people. Don't curtail him just because he has to be like other boys his age.

Setting up expectations that your son may not be able to live up to can only make him feel incompetent and unworthy at some point. Instead, praise him for his choices and his efforts because your assurance can give a tremendous boost to his confidence.

I must admit that there have been times when I felt rather frustrated and even slightly hurt while dealing with my teenage boys. I'm certain that all other parents might have also experienced this at some point or another. In my bid to be a better parent, I might have unknowingly done things that strained my relationship with my boys. In this section, let us look at certain common parenting mistakes that must be avoided while dealing with teenagers.

If you want your bond to stay strong, then you need to make certain changes to your parenting style. While talking to your teenage son, do you ever talk to him as if he was still a child? It's not only about what you're saying, but the way you talk too. You need to understand that your child is moving towards adulthood. If you keep talking to him as if he's still a child, it will only frustrate him more. Even if you don't agree with what he is saying, it is important to start treating him like an adult and listen to what he's saying. Everyone wants to be heard, and your son wants the same. Parents often complain that it feels as though their child doesn't respect them. Well, respect is a two-way street. If you treat your teenager with respect, then he will reciprocate.

Do you ever treat a conversation with your son like it is an obligation or a chore you need to complete? If yes, then he can perceive this, and he will be hurt.

Understand that he is no longer a child but is maturing into an adult. I don't mean that you must not occasionally lecture your child or focus on his behavior. Instead, ensure that a majority of your conversations are about connecting with him and forming a bond.

Most parents tend to multitask while talking to their kids. However, try your best to avoid this. If your son is talking to you and your multitasking, it sends a message that what he's saying isn't that important. You're inadvertently conveying that he doesn't deserve your full attention. So, the next time you're talking to your teenage son, ensure that you give him your undivided attention.

At times, parents tend to try too hard. Don't try to force a conversation and let it flow naturally. Also, ensure that you don't interrupt your son while he is talking. Let him finish, and then you can talk.

Dealing with a Teen

You might not realize it, but your teen's behavior is also related to the way you parent him. Maintaining a good relationship with your teen will help him feel happier and more content with life. In this section, you will learn about simple tips that will come in handy while dealing with your kids. These tips are practical and easy to follow. Also, they will help reduce any conflicts or tension too.

Be a parent as well as a friend

A common mistake that a lot of parents make is that they are either a strict parent or a close friend to their teens. However, you must find a middle ground. All teens desire to be understood by their parents, appreciated by them, and loved for who they are. Not just this, but they also desire a lot of independence and freedom. Don't think that by being a friend, your teen will not respect you. Don't you cherish and respect your friends? It is about establishing healthy boundaries. It is about being a good parent and a friend to your teen. Make the atmosphere in the home conducive of healthy discussions. Create an environment where your teen can talk to you about all his worries.

Spend time together

You need to spend at least a couple of minutes every day talking to your teen. It doesn't have to be about anything specific. Just check in on your teen and ask him how his day was and if he is fine. You can set up a small routine. Maybe you can talk to him for a couple of minutes before he goes to sleep every night or talk to him once he is back from school. It is merely a way of staying in touch with your teen. Also, it encourages him to start talking about what's going on in his life.

Appropriate parenting

If you don't want to or refuse to acknowledge the fact that your son is growing up, it will only invite conflict. Understand that he is growing and that his needs will change. Your son will naturally want more freedom. However, this doesn't mean that you have to be scared about asking him where he's going or whom he's going out with. It is a good idea to get to know your son's friends and parents too. Don't be hesitant in asking for these details. However, while doing this, ensure that you don't indulge in overparenting. Don't be a hovering parent and instead give him his freedom. You can certainly set certain restrictions on that freedom, provided that they are reasonable. If they are reasonable, then your son will comply with them.

Manage your expectations

Your son will obviously want to be his best self. As a parent, it is your duty to ensure that he can do this. You need to support your child in his endeavor to be his best self. However, this doesn't mean that you start setting goals that you want him to accomplish. Instead, work along with your teen and try to understand what he wants. Once you understand this, it becomes easier to set goals that he can work toward. Try to support your teen. Even if you don't understand what he wants right away, spend some time with him, talk to him, and you will soon understand. Remember that your teen is seeking your approval; even his behavior doesn't convey this.

So, if you set unrealistic expectations for him, he might be scared that he will disappoint you. All this will only frustrate him and make him feel anxious.

Mealtime

Make it a point that you have at least one meal with your son daily. It can be breakfast or dinner. As long as you both share a meal, it gives you the perfect opportunity to open up communication. Try to make it a point that you eat as many meals together as a family as you possibly can. This will certainly have a positive effect on the way your teen feels about himself and his family. If he can see the family as one unit, he will feel more secure and relaxed. Also, this is a perfect way to unwind and stay in touch with the happenings of each other's lives.

Communication is quintessential

It is important to keep the lines of communication with your teen clear and open at all times. He must not be scared to talk to you about things. However, at the same time, he must not take this liberty for granted. You need to get down to his level and talk to him as his peers would, while being a good parent. Learning to communicate efficiently and effectively will help reduce the chances of any miscommunication. Also, it will help strengthen your relationship.

Don't ignore self-care

Leading by example is a great way to go about parenting a teen. If you live a healthy life and your teen sees you doing the same, it might give him the inspiration to follow in your footsteps. Make sure that you get plenty of sleep, eat a balanced diet, and do things that make you happy. When your teen sees you do all of this, he will naturally be inclined to do the same. By promoting self-care, your teen will start to feel better about himself.

Independence

Yes, your teen will want a lot of independence. However, don't try to push independence on him if he is not ready yet. Some teens take a while longer to step out of the nest. It is okay. Don't push him into anything that he is scared of. Be there to nurture and guide him. Allow your teen to understand that you are there for him.

By following these simple steps, you can certainly improve the relationship you share with your teen.

Chapter 7: Getting Communication Right

We identified that successful relationships are the most important element in maintaining happiness throughout life and of course the relationships between parents and their children are a very important part of this. For many parents, the relationships with their teenage children seem to become increasingly difficult. Some of this is a natural breaking of the bonds of dependency that teenagers need to go through before they reach adulthood, but many of the problems are made worse by poor communication between parents and teens. Parents see their teenage children as poor communicators, who don't listen, show little interest in having meaningful conversations with their parents and often seem incapable of expressing more than a few words or grunts in response to questions. In fact, it is often we the parents, who are the poor communicators and need help to learn more effective communication skills and not just our children.

When we are dealing with our younger children, even if we feel like we are giving them encouragement and support, much of the time we are issuing instructions to ensure that they behave in the way we want them to and to keep them safe. We take for granted that we know best and that we will always have the final say on what they can and can't do. Unfortunately, we find it very difficult to change this style of communication, even though our children are changing dramatically. Our teenagers therefore often come to see us as people, who don't listen to them, don't respect their opinions and as being unresponsive to whatever they say.

So, if we are to improve our communications with our teenagers, we have to start to change our ways to ensure that our communication is a two-way process. It is worth looking back on your communication with your teenager over the course of the day and considering how much was shared conversation and how much was instruction or advice giving.

Plan opportunities to communicate

Start by recognizing that having meaningful conversations with teenagers is not easy and you'll have to do a bit of planning. It can be helpful if you create some windows of opportunity when both parties are not likely to be distracted by other things. This will depend entirely on the schedules of the individuals themselves and how the family functions. It may be when they first return from school; it may be during a shared meal at home or elsewhere or it may be during a regular car journey. Your attempts may not always be very successful but keep trying. Make sure that you know as much as possible about what is going on in your teenager's life both inside and outside of the home and show a consistent interest in their affairs, even if they don't seem to want you to!

Be a good questioner

Learn to be a good questioner. This means finding out more about what your teenager thinks by gently, calmly and tactfully asking them. It is much better with teenagers to always try to use "open" questions, that is questions that cannot be answered with a simple yes or no such as:

How do you feel school went today?

What do you think you can do to improve things?

Why do you feel like that?

What do you suggest we should do?

What will happen if you do that?

How can we best support you?

How will you know if you made the right decision?

How will you notice if things get better?

Be a good listener

It's vital that you learn to be a good listener. That means giving the conversation your complete attention and looking at your teenager. Letting them talk and take as long as possible to say it. Not interrupting or trying to add to or finish what they are saying. Showing that you are listening with appropriate nods and body language and whatever is said trying not to take it personally and keeping calm. Remember that you have two ears and one mouth, and good listening comes from using those in proportion!

Be a good responder

Learning to be a good responder is another very useful skill. That means showing that you have heard and understood what has been said. If necessary, repeat back what you think has been said or try to summarise and make sure that is what was meant. Take stock, by looking and listening, and consider the emotional state of mind of your teenager and try to respond to that.

You don't have to agree with your teenager, but by validating their position, you show that you accept what they are saying and are trying to understand it. If you dismiss or ignore what they are saying or try to minimise something which may be very important to them at this moment, it will not promote good communication. Try not to judge them and do not call them silly or stupid or wrong.

Sometimes the only response that a teenager may need is a bit of empathy, but, on other occasions, you may need to help them identify solutions to their own problems. Go through the options with them and get them to identify the pros and cons of the various approaches. You may need to discuss issues that involve moral judgements and ethics and you need to recognise that they probably live in a world with different ideas of what is normal or acceptable than you. It is important that you justify your position by explaining it, even though they may not accept it. Try to be as honest and open as possible. Remember the aim is to encourage independent solution finding and not necessarily to fix their problems.

Involve your teenager in household problem solving

Sometimes you could involve teenagers in helping you find solutions to your own, or household problems and seek their advice and contributions whenever there is an opportunity. Teenagers are often great at giving advice about computers and technical issues. They may not appreciate all the financial implications of what they say, but this is a good opportunity to encourage their involvement. They are also likely to have a view on family holiday locations, what cars to buy and many other issues in the home. Listen to them and don't ignore their ideas. If you accept them say so, and if you don't say why not. Try not to instantly dismiss ideas with a "yes but." and don't be overcommitted to your own pre-conceived ideas.

Hopefully, by following the above guidance, you will find that over time your level of communication with your teenager improves. You will notice that the above guidelines are about conversations, which are not argumentative or confrontational, but where the emphasis is on identifying possible solutions together. We will deal with these later, but you will find if you improve the lines of communication in general, that arguments and conflicts may be reduced.

Don't be a bad boss

As a final thought, think about all the bad bosses that you might have had. Bad bosses are usually categorized by three main faults:

They tell you to do things without explaining why

They never praise or give you credit for what you do right

They never listen to your point of view

As parents, we need to try to make sure that we do not treat our teenagers like this!

Chapter 8: Establishing Teenage Rights, Privileges And Responsibilities

The culture of entitlement among teenagers is widespread and can be extremely damaging in later life and so it is essential that parents can distinguish between their teenager's rights and privileges. In fact, the rights that teenagers should expect are quite limited:

- The right to live in a safe physical and emotional space
- The right to adequate food, clothing, shelter
- The right to be loved, valued and treated with respect

Teenagers do not generally have the right to any of the following privileges, although they may sometimes be necessary for safety or health purposes:

- Expensive clothes
- Special diets or meal times
- Parental taxi service
- Money for non-essentials
- Access or ownership of phones/computers

Even more importantly, as we shall discuss shortly, teenagers should not expect to be protected from disappointments and hardships, or to not having to contribute towards the functioning of the household.

Teenagers are very egocentric and often find it hard to see other peoples' point of view. The logic of a teenager's sense of entitlement goes something like this. If I want something badly enough it is a parent's duty to give it to me as otherwise, I will be really upset. Unfortunately, many parents and other involved adults collude with this approach. They indulge their teenagers to demonstrate how much they love them, and to avoid arguments and disappointments, and convince themselves that they are maximising their children's opportunities and happiness. They overpraise and over-reward normal behaviour and overprotect them from the consequences of their actions. As a result, they achieve the exact opposite of what they intend. Rather than developing successful and happy adults, they create self-centred people who have unrealistic expectations and are likely to meet considerable disappointment. They are embedding attitudes that most adults struggle with including:

Poor impulse and emotional control

Poor coping skills

Lack of perseverance

Poor resilience

Lack of self-discipline

Low self esteem

So, what should I be doing instead?

The following are strategies that might be employed. As usual, it is better if these begin before the teenage years, but it is never too late to start.

Be prepared to reject, postpone or negotiate your teenager's demands

No matter how much anger it may cause, you should always be prepared to reject a demand if you think it is undeserved, unnecessary or unaffordable. Your teenager needs to learn that in life you do not always get what you want. As far as possible, you should explain your reasoning, even if they don't accept it.

It is often a good idea to delay or postpone a demand. Teenagers need to realise that they can't always have instant gratification. You might say they can have it for their birthday or Christmas present, or that they can have it when the old one is no longer suitable.

Lastly, you may wish to try to negotiate a solution with your teenager. This may involve saving up or doing paid jobs for you or someone else or possibly selling something that they already have. These are good opportunities to develop problem solving techniques as well as the skills of money management.

Give your teenager responsibility for themselves

As far as possible you should encourage your teenager to take responsibility for looking after themselves. They should be responsible for their own hygiene, cleaning their room and sorting out their laundry. They need to steadily take over organising themselves both for their school and domestic requirements, so that they become skilled in time management and setting priorities. They also need to develop money management skills. Giving them an allowance is a good idea, but it must be clear what it is or is not meant to pay for. It should also be clear that once it is spent, it will not normally be topped up.

Give your teenager responsibility to the household and to others

Your teenager needs to learn early that the world won't revolve around them and that families and society in general, are two-way processes of give and take. Provide as many opportunities as you can for them to take responsibility for some general household duties, so that they can make their contribution to the running of the household. This is also a good opportunity to teach them domestic skills such as doing the vacuuming, doing the laundry, cleaning bathrooms etc.

Encourage your teenager to help other people. Volunteering to help children with disabilities, deprived families or old neighbours helps teenagers develop empathy and a better understanding of other people. It reduces the obsession with themselves and can lead to greater gratitude of their own circumstances.

Stop rescuing your teenager

Your teenager ought to learn to be responsible for their own actions and to take the consequences. They should be made to pay for damages caused to other people's property and to apologise for bad behaviour. Hard as it might be, for you and for them, they need to learn from their mistakes. If this seems unkind, just consider how long you want to wear that superhero cape! They will learn from experience, but if you keep rescuing your child from the consequences of his decisions, or lack of thinking ahead, you are robbing him of valuable lessons that will stick with him for the rest of his life.

Stop shielding your teenager

Think about the moment that you first discovered that life is tough and often unfair! It was a hard lesson, but a necessary one. Your teenager must be allowed to make mistakes and deal with their own failures. They also should be allowed to take more risks and move out of their comfort zones, if they are to develop independence. Where appropriate, include and let them be involved in discussions about family problems including work, health or financial challenges.

Enforce boundaries and expectations

If your teenager misbehaves or ignores boundaries, there need to be consequences. Once you are clear in your mind (and theirs) what their privileges are, it is much easier to impose sanctions or instigate rewards. Your teenager will continue to make bad choices and persist in negative behaviour until the pain that comes from those decisions outweighs the perceived benefits.

Praise appropriately

Too many parents overpraise their children in a bid to boost their self-confidence. Praise is good, but only when it is linked to the right activities. Activities that involve hard work and perseverance are certainly praiseworthy, as are helping others or making a valuable contribution to the household. Try to encourage your teenager to feel pride in their own behaviour, rather than just responding to your reaction. Rather than saying "I'm proud of you for that", try to encourage them to reflect on their own feelings about their achievements:

"How did you feel knowing that you had achieved that?"

"You should feel really proud of that"

We need to develop teenagers who achieve and behave well for their own sake and not for the approval of other individuals. Reliance on other peoples' approval can lead to problems as it assumes that other peoples' expectations are justified and correct. It may also make it difficult for teenagers to say no to others when they should.

Be consistent

All the adults who are closely involved with your teenager need to be working in a co-ordinated and consistent fashion. This includes parents, step-parents, grandparents and others. It is no good for teenagers having requests refused if they just go elsewhere for them. This becomes difficult in families where divorce or marital breakdown leads to one or the other parent point scoring. In the ideal scenario, both parents would agree to abide by the same ground rules, talk, reason and negotiate for a solution that works. But the emphasis here is on agreeing what course of action to take to ensure that your teenager is very clear about sanctions and consequences.

Chapter 9: Managing Fear and Risk

There are those among us who are more risk takers and those who do what they can to minimize their exposure to risk. You can be a risk taker when it comes to climbing mountains, investing in stocks, or trying new things, but may be risk avoidant when it comes to being honest with others.

You could be willing to share your personal truths with others but afraid to be alone.

You could be afraid of heights, planes, snakes, spiders, or shadows in the night but willing to tell your child the truth about your adolescence.

We all are afraid of something. Sometime. Sooner or later something fearful will come your way.

We show it differently and handle it differently but we all get to deal with fear. Some know fear more than others, but no one gets to avoid it entirely.

There can be moments of fear in every day. You can hear a noise, have a meeting with the boss, not hear from your child, or feel something in your life is amiss. Small fears may register a 1 or 2 on your emotional Richter scale, some larger ones might come in at a 5 or 7, and the really big ones can take you right up to the top of the scale.

You never know what is going to cause those rumbles to become tumbles. There are things you wouldn't necessarily think would evoke a fearful reaction that could come along and catch you off guard. You could be thinking everything is fine and then the phone rings and you hear something that could significantly affect your life. You might get off that phone very afraid. Or elated. Or sad. Or mad. The phone rings and with it comes the unknown.

Let's just say you wanted to better handle the stressful, fearful times in your life. And let's just say you asked me what I thought you could do that would build up your navigation skills when fear crossed your path.

I wish there was a formula I could give you that could guarantee solid results. I wish I could provide that level of hope. Unfortunately, I can't point to any tried-and-true formula that has been time-tested and has glowing reviews.

What I can offer is an exercise regime which, like most regimes, is destined to not be fully followed. But see what you can do.

- Take small risks.

- Do little things that most probably will be of little consequence.

I am sorry to say this, but it is true. If you want to get better at dealing with fear you need to deal with more of it, not less. You are not going to build your skills without exercising them. There are plenty of unexpected tense situations that will come your way and fear will come with them. You can't control what the world deals you, so you might as well build your skills.

You can be proactive and choose to take small risks where you experience a low level of fear. You can build your confidence like any other muscle by starting small and building. Something happens and you feel that initial wave of fear in your body. You can ask yourself, what exactly is scaring you and what low-risk thing could you do to try to reduce that fear? Then you can choose to do it or not.

If you want to do some self-therapy you could pick a time during the day when you could take a few moments to reflect back on the day and scan for those fear/chance-taking moments. Think about the actions taken and not taken. See if you can acknowledge to yourself the efforts you made regardless of the results.

One time in the heyday of my bachelor life I saw a very attractive woman across the room and wanted to meet her. I didn't know anyone there and I knew if it was going to happen I would have to walk across the room and say hello.

I was too afraid to say hello, afraid of being awkward, her rejecting me, and me feeling not worthy enough to be with someone like that.

So I drove home in a funk. I was not happy with myself for not taking a chance and speaking with her. Sure, I could have fumbled my words and she might have laughed at me and told me to get lost. (I am a "think of the worst and hope for the best" kind of guy.)

But I didn't let that happen. I rejected myself. I didn't even give myself a chance.

I didn't like that and I told myself that from then on I was going to let other people reject me and not have me do it for them. I have not batted 100% with that decision, but I have upped my batting average. Even though it hurts when someone rejects me, I would rather they do it than I do it.

In many ways I now fear rejecting myself more than I do others rejecting me.

Fear takes many forms—fear of flying, failure, the list goes on. Fear can limit activity. My fear of rejection kept me from taking a chance and speaking with the woman across the room. Many of the things others do without much effort requires some people to scale a giant wall of fear.

Most children have a little anxiety when they first start school and have to leave their family. Most soon get comfortable and going to school is no big thing, except when there is a test or some other unpleasantry waiting. Some children really don't want to go to school and going requires a lot of parental support and creates a high dose of anxiety all around.

Every year I receive at least one call from a parent who is having difficulty getting their child out of bed. They cajole, they bribe, they threaten, they withhold, then they call. Unfortunately there usually is not an easy fix. Working at a private school we have some leeway in how we approach these situations. Usually we set up some one-step-at-a-time kind of protocol where we have the student make small inroads into coming to school. If it is too much to do a whole day, how about part of a day? How about they come and visit school when no one is there? We have to tailor-make a plan with the child so she can take on her fear in bite size pieces.

Most parents have difficulty dealing with their child's fears because the child's fear activates the parent's fear. If their child won't go to school then they won't get into a good college and then their life will be ruined. Albert Ellis, PhD called this 'horribilizing'. We take one event and then run with it to its most horrible conclusion. He advises focusing at the moment at hand and not letting your fear run rampant.

Parents want to stabilize events to minimize their own fear. When your child's life is not going the way you want it to go, emotions get triggered. Parents get worried, they get angry, they blame themselves, they blame the child or the school, and they are afraid.

At first, they usually don't talk about their fear. They just act on it.

You might want to consider speaking about what you are concerned and worried about. At least initially to the other parent. Whether you are afraid that if your daughter doesn't go to school she will end up not having a valuable life or afraid that whatever caused her to do what she is doing is not reversible, your fear is going to prompt you to do something. Your child may not hear the cause of your fear, but she will sense your fear. Which then will make her afraid.

Parents are supposed to be fear soothers not fear enhancers. If you speak to your child about what you are afraid of it will allow your child to respond directly to your fear. If you just come at her with your consequence-laden emotional tirade it will only spawn an argument.

The more you know about what you are afraid of and can share it with others the more able they will be to assist you. While your child's response to your worry may not fully soothe you, you will at least have gotten the real issue on the table. Your daughter may think your fear is irrational and you may think her behavior is unacceptable, but at least now you are focused on the core of the issue.

Most people would rather not think about the things that provoke their fear. Thinking about scary things can scare you. Yet, avoiding your fear is not going to help you deal with it any better. You will be able to improve your ability to handle your own fears if you make an effort to think about yourself and fear every day. You don't have to do anything. Just reflect on the role of fear in your day and how you respond to it. As you get more comfortable acknowledging fear, you will also become aware of your responses to it and begin to explore other ways to manage those things that cause you worry.

Here is a two-part homework assignment:

1. Every day for the next week set aside 5 minutes to allow yourself time to quietly focus on how fear has involved itself in your day and how you have responded to it.

2. Every day for a week in some way do something you are fearful of, something that raises a small caution flag. Find small opportunities to stretch yourself. Just a little.

Regardless of how your risk-taking activity pans out you need to reward yourself for having taken the chance. The goal here is not so much to take chances and do fearful things so that you win prizes or praises—although you might.

The goal is to become more comfortable facing your fears. Whether you are just thinking about them or doing something about them. There will be fearful items that you think about that you will chose not to face. Okay, those items are too loaded to take on now. Instead of beating up on yourself for what you are not doing, consider rewarding yourself for what you are doing.

If I had made it a point to go up to an attractive women each day for a week and initiate a conversation I am sure it would have built up my courage and ability. Instead I took what I could have learned in a week and extended it over a year.

Sure there will be things that you remain fearful of. Jumping out of a burning building will probably always be fearful. But talking honestly with your child or facing some other less life-threatening fears ought to become easier as you allow yourself to attempt those things that give you a little fear. You can walk across the room and introduce yourself or go out to dinner alone or tackle something with less fear than you previously held.

Practice taking small risks. Reward yourself regardless of what you did and how you did it. Tomorrow will provide you more opportunities. You won't bat 1000, but don't let that stop you from coming to bat.

Try it for a week. Or two. Or as long as you like.

Of course if you focus on fear you will become more aware of it. This is a two-sided coin. You might be more blissfully unaware of how much fear you hold before you attend more to its presence. Yet that awareness will allow you to consciously put effort into reducing the fear. Just because you may not consciously be aware of how much fear you are holding does not mean it isn't there. Fear will motivate you whether it is conscious or not. You might as well know what it is triggering you and how it is affecting your life. With that increase in awareness you will gain the ability to make more conscious choices about how to proceed.

It is risky facing fear.

Almost as risky as not.

Chapter 10: Security and Lies

A sense of security is something we all need. When we feel safe in our home, our work, and our world, we rarely think about how good it feels to be safe. We just comfortably accept that we don't have to worry about something. Sadly, we don't always get to feel safe. When our own sense of security is threatened it adds a lot of stress to our lives.

When parents are struggling with their relationship, finances, health or anything else that might dislodge the structure of the home, children get anxious. As do parents. That stress is not healthy for anyone and the longer it invades a home the less secure everyone will feel. Uncertainty, while it can have its moments, can also add layers of stress to a situation.

Ideally we are secure about ourselves and our ability to make a "successful", meaningful, valuable life. But most of us have some insecurity about that. We do not know the future. We can have hopes and beliefs and good odds. But with that we also have uncertainty, human frailty and no guarantees aside from taxes and death.

Many of the people I know are a few paydays away from having considerable financial unrest. We manage our lives as best we can, but there are a lot of people who have worried at one time or another about whether they might be homeless or underemployed. Many people are homeless or underemployed. Many people are one doctor visit away from disturbing news that could disrupt their life. Many couples are one good argument away from ending their partnership.

Security, as important as it is, is temporary.

We know life is not fair and shit happens. We just hope not too much of it comes our way and what does come we can resolve relatively easily.

A parent wants their child to not have to worry about the roof over his head or the food in his stomach. But there is a distressing amount of people in the world that worry about these things every day. The more difficult your financial, health, or other destabilizing situation, the more you need to let your child know you:

a) Love him.

b) Want the best for him.

c) Believe in his ability to better his circumstances.

You don't ever want your discomfort with the turn your life has taken to cause you to lash out at your child and say "You will never be any good" or "You will never amount to anything."

Those kinds of comments are not good motivators for most people. They do get some children to rise up and prove you wrong, but statistically they become better predictors than motivators. If your life is not going the way you would like, it does not mean you need to curse your child with the same affliction. If you are disappointed in your life, spend time coming to your own place of acceptance and work on managing your life in more rewarding ways.

Hurting and handicapping your child because you're hurt is not a model for making the world a better place. Deal with your own situation in your own way, but deal with the parenting of your child in a way that is best for your child.

If your life is unstable then your child will adapt and learn to live in that instability. I had a sophomore tell me that this was the tenth school he had been to and as a consequence he was very able to make new friends. Keeping them, he told me, was something he didn't know much about, but by necessity he had learned how to reach out to others.

While learning how to deal with instability is a life skill we all need to learn, I think people get plenty of that in their lifetime and you don't need to add to it if you don't have to. If you are in the midst of a divorce or health/financial issues, everyone in the family will need to learn how to handle it. So be it. It is hard enough dealing with those kinds of issues; please don't beat up on yourself or others for being in the situation. Save your energy for figuring how to best resolve the situation.

While shit happens that you often cannot control, you are the model for how to handle it. The better a job you do of dealing with whatever happens, the easier it will be for everyone else. I don't want to make you feel guilty if you are not managing your life so well at the moment. I do know life can deal out some extreme blows that do humble us and our bouncing back resiliency is not always as robust as we would like.

I am a believer that if something big is going on it is best to tell your children. He will pick up on the felt change in things and will react but not understand why. Putting a name and a story to what is happening helps a family share and support each other. Being open eliminates some secrets and allows people to more openly share their experience. Which usually brings people closer. We have all witnessed horrible catastrophes and seen people come together in ways they would not have done if events were more usual. Invest in the power of your family and sharing together the truth of your life.

Sharing with your children that your relationship with your partner is challenging right now or your money situation is not as you would like it to be or your health is not in good shape is not an easy conversation to have. You want to be in as calm a place as you can be, because once you start talking emotions are likely to start flaring up. For you and everyone else.

Feelings are going to come out sooner or later. It is a good idea when you decide to speak with your child about something that is liable to be unsettling to start by saying, "There is something we all need to talk about. I want to make sure we all talk about this and join together in dealing with it." Then I would lead with the facts and the emotions will follow.

A loud family shouting match can send everyone to their corners. A good family cry will bring everyone closer. Sometimes you have one before the other. Ideally I would prefer you keep the shouting and name-calling for when you are alone. Then go ahead and vent away.

When you share something, others want to know how you are dealing with it and what you are going to do. Children especially want to know how their parents are going to deal with a destabilizing event. They want to know that everything is going to be okay. It is hard to give that reassurance when you are not sure yourself. I encourage you to seek out within yourself the belief that no matter how badly things turn out, ultimately everything comes to homeostasis.

I don't like to give this example but it is a worst case scenario that underscores this point. If you are not well and don't have long to live, that certainly is destabilizing for everyone. Your family will be operating in crisis mode and it will be hard for you to give the message that ultimately everything will be all right. And yet, even though you will not be present and you do know at some level there will be a great loss for your family and the wounds of that loss may last a lifetime, everyone will eventually find their way to laughter and joy and the ability to make their lives happy and meaningful. I don't know if your death will be comforting for you or not. It depends on a lot of matters, but as sad as it may be there may be some comfort for you in knowing your children will survive and ultimately be okay. You can give them that reassurance.

That is a worst case scenario and hopefully you are not facing that. Pretty much everything will in due course resolve itself and a new status quo will evolve. I would want my child to know that while things are not as I would want them in this moment, I believe in our family's ability to navigate these waters and arrive at safer, calmer shores.

Knowledge is calming. Even if it is alarming.

Uncertainty is more nerve wracking.

Having a plan, even one that may need to be reevaluated right away, gives a sense of security in uncertain times. We all like to have control. Plans, even plans you may not fully believe in, usually lessen anxiety. Less anxiety, more security.

My bottom line is this:

Do your best to make your children feel as secure as possible, as loved as possible, as believed in as possible and as trusted as possible.

And enjoy him and your time with him. For many people the years raising their children are considered the best years of their lives. Strife and all.

Lying

I would be lying if I said I didn't believe everyone lies. Some more than others. Some bigger than others. Sometimes to others and sometimes to ourselves.

Lying is a life skill. You need it to survive in this world. I am not happy about that, but as far as I can tell it is a necessity.

Of course there are all manner of lies.

There are the ones you tell your kids when they ask about Santa Claus, your sexual and drug history, and the truth about what really happened before and after you met their other parent.

There are the ones your child tells you when you ask where she went, what she was doing, and if she was drinking or doing drugs.

Parents have a low tolerance for the lies their children tell and high tolerance for their own. Most everyone has more tolerance for their own lies than they do for anyone else's. We usually can find the justification for our lies, and while we may understand the reasoning behind our child's lie, we still would prefer she tell the truth.

Children grow up to be able to discern most of the lies their parents tell. Yes, we all want to believe we can fool some of the people some of the time and indeed we can. If you happen to be charged to teaching your child that honesty is most usually the best policy you will need to model that value. The double standard you might hold about withholding your personal history, while it may get supporters when your child is young, loses importance as your child grows up. It may be okay and advisable to not tell your budding teenager about your misbegotten youth. You might want to save that for when she has established stronger connections to her own values about how to live her life.

I am sure most parents don't always walk the walk they are talking to their child. You may not be that into physical fitness for yourself but you may be encouraging and supporting your child to stay fit. Certainly she will realize sooner or later that your words and actions don't always go hand-in-hand. You may talk the talk but get caught not walking the walk. While that may not be your proudest moment as a parent, you are teaching her a lesson that she will run into time and again in the world. Might as well start to get used to it with you. But hopefully not too often.

If you are going to be extolling something to your child that you do not do you might as well come clean and share that with your child. You have reasons why you do and don't do what you do and don't do. They may not be the best reasons, but they are yours. They may be illogical or they may make perfect sense. Sharing why you do what you do and being willing to talk about it are the kinds of conversations you might want your child to have with you.

I know there are lies that are best kept to yourself. Or so it seems to you. It very well may be for the best to keep your truth to yourself. Or not. It is not always easy to predict what will be for the best in the moment and in the long run. Which is why people withhold the truth. Still, despite the possible advantages to lying, most parents say they want their child to grow up to be honest.

But do they really?

Parents want their children to learn how to tell small social lies that are commonplace in our society. When someone asks us how we are we know they don't really want to know so we lie and say, "Fine." Children learn the socially polite things to say. They even get rewarded for it. When your child thanks her grandmother for the generous and thoughtful gift that has everyone smirking, the parents slip a nod of approval to the child.

Most parents want their child to learn how to be polite and respectful even if it means leaving the truth behind. They just don't want their children to lie to them about the things that are important to them. Things that have to do with school, drugs, sex, and saying she is fine when she is not even close.

The "I did my homework" when she didn't is a lie most parents don't like to hear.

Since we all want to believe we can fool some of the people some of the time, and would prefer some of our behaviors go unnoticed, we gauge the risk/reward and at times choose to lay low and hope we get away with it.

Your child wants to be able to fool you. You want to be able to fool her.

You also want to be able to catch her most (if not all) of the time when she is fooling you. I am sure there are some advantages to occasionally letting her slip something by you. Especially if it is not a big ticket item. But, I would prefer she learn that it isn't all that worth it to withhold the truth and carry the burden of lying.

What do you think your fielding percentage is on catching the lies your child tells? _____

I would imagine most parents have a good sense of the degree to which their child lies to them. I have yet to meet the parent who thought their child was 100% honest about everything in their life. Well, that is not true. I have met those parents. But their kids were not yet in their teens.

From listening to students I have come to believe that once you get to be 13 you have a pretty good understanding of what you need to lie about to your parents. Your child will see how you react to certain events and if she suspects she is not going to get a positive reception she may choose to bend the truth, omit the truth, or clam up.

As your child grows up and develops her own sense of self, she will want to retain certain things just for herself. Keeping a part of her day or life to herself empowers her, while at the same time it disengages her from you. Her quest for autonomy will prompt her to want to keep certain things from you. It is not so much lying to you as being her own counsel. When she figures she can handle something, whatever it is, she might opt for taking care of the situation without you ever knowing. As we all know, sometimes that works out okay and sometimes it doesn't.

Some things you will never know, some you will suspect and some you might be better off not knowing. I would prefer your child tell you she does not want to share something with you than lie to you about it. While you might not be happy to hear this, your acceptance of her desire to withhold some truth lets her know you trust her ability to take care of matters. Your actions demonstrate faith in her, even though you might prefer knowing everything. That is the kind of endorsement teenagers need.

Certainly if things go south there will need to be a follow-up discussion where you will hopefully endeavor to keep your "I told you so" to yourself. You can be empathetic, disappointed, and full of questions and, if asked, ideas about how to proceed. When things don't work out for your child, you usually don't need to rub it in too much.

I tell students and parents that the contract I would want between a parent and their child is for everyone to share the significant truths in their lives with the family. I would want everyone to be forthcoming about those matters that they know are of considerable concern to others. It is okay to keep some truths to yourself, but the ones you know would affect others are the ones that need to be shared.

It is akin to when a parent needs to have surgery and they debate whether to tell their child before or after or never. Most children I have spoken with have told me they would want to know. Yes, they don't really want to know and worry, but if something is happening that could potentially be life threatening they wanted to know sooner than later. Of course, some children would rather not know. You might want to have a family discussion and ask what everyone thinks and wants.

I would want my child to tell me when she was more than the usual amount of afraid or anxious and the circumstances in her life were starting to shift not for the better. I would also want to know when things were picking up. I don't need to know the day-to-day although I would like to, but I really would like to know about any shifts. I would offer to provide that for her as well if she would like.

When parents discover their child has lied to them it does bring with it a shadow. There is a tendency to be a little more distrusting. If she lied about this one thing perhaps she is lying about something else as well.

Getting back the trust to a pre-lie state in which your child was held in higher trust can take time. Some relationships never get back there. Others can get back to an even higher level.

It is a funny thing about trust. Some people are more trusting and others not so much. Some people can easily brush off a lie and others are deeply impacted. There are many variables at play. Most parents start off fully trusting their child and over time learn what to trust and what to not ask about. Of course, your child started off fully trusting you and has had to learn to live with your imperfections.

Regardless of your fielding average catching her in the lies she tries to get past you, you are better served trusting that she will tell you the truth. That alone will not decrease her lying. But it won't increase it either. If you can combine that trust with a general trust in her ability to manage her life then her need to lie diminishes even more. She knows you believe that even if she screwed up big time, you believe in her ability to clean it up. She also knows you would prefer she didn't screw things up that much.

Regardless of how much you trust or don't trust your child, I am going to try to raise that level.

Let's once again start with you. If you want your child to be more truthful with you there are two things to consider:

1. Are you willing to raise your own level of honesty?

2. How do you reward her honesty and discipline her lies?

How honest are you with your child about:

- Your hopes for her?

- Your feelings/thoughts about her accomplishments?

- Your feelings/thoughts about her disappointments?

- Your hopes for your life and what has happened to them?

- Your feelings/thoughts about your accomplishments & disappointments?

- Your beliefs about lying?

- Your experiences with lying when you were on the giving and receiving end?

- Your experiences with lying when you chose to lie to someone you cared about?

- Your experiences of lying to your parents?

- Your experiences of lying to your child?

Would you be willing to initiate a discussion with your teenager about those items? If not all, some?

What do you think would be the upside and the downside?

_____
_____
_____
_____
____

If you decide to initiate a discussion don't deluge her with your truths. I would have them come out in bits and pieces over time. Even if you shared all your truths about those items, she may not share anything. While you are hoping you can create an ongoing discussion about these items, there is no telling if she will want to participate.

If she elects not to share her own truths what will you do?

Will you share your disappointment with her not sharing? Will you say something provocative to get her talking? Will you cop an attitude and say something to end the moment with a bad taste in everyone's mouth? Or will you let her know that you are pleased that you shared more of your truths and she listened and anytime she wants to pick up the conversation you are happy to do so?

Whenever you disclose something you are going to have a reaction to the other person's reaction. Sometimes you share it and sometimes you don't. If you were being completely honest about everything all the time your reaction to their reaction to your reaction to their reaction could keep you on a treadmill you can't get out of fast enough.

Honestly you could be mad, sad, glad, and scared. And honestly you might want to share some of that, none of that, or all of that.

When you are being honest you do it because it makes you feel good about you. Don't do something in expectation of the response. Sure, you can hope your modeling will be inspiring to her, but how your sharing affects her is up to her.

You model the behavior you believe in and leave it at that. A step at a time. And remember, this is the time in her life that she needs to disengage from you so she is liable to share less with you than you might like.

Let me introduce you to the concept of Successive Approximation.

If you wanted to teach your young child to memorize the alphabet you probably would not expect her to be able to hear it once and repeat it back correctly. You might hope she got the ABC part and yet whenever she veered off course you would either say nothing or gently remind her what came next. You might even do this for a few minutes one day and then again another. You might even sing it along with her until one day she gets the whole thing and you might say, "You really worked hard on that to learn it. Well done."

Each time your child tries to recite the alphabet and doesn't get it perfectly right it is called an approximation. She is approximating the desired final behavior. If she tries more than once it is called a successive approximation.

In the psychology research labs they run various experiments that basically prove if you reward the approximations it hastens the arrival at the goal. If you only reward the accomplishment of the final goal it decreases the odds of getting to the final goal.

People need encouragement along the way. Here is the example I often share with parents:

You want your child to keep her room tidy because you no longer can stand not seeing her floor. You buy her a laundry hamper and put it in her room and ask her to please put her dirty clothes in the hamper.

You walk in the next day and the floor looks a lot like it did the day before. But you notice there is a sock that must have been thrown in the general direction of the hamper as it is now resting half on the floor and half on the side of the hamper.

You say, "I'm glad to see the sock almost made it to the hamper. Well done."

Then you leave.

I know you could be having a fair amount of reactions to that approach and I wouldn't argue with most of them. Yet if you go into her room every day and point at something that almost made it to the hamper or made it in the hamper or was at least in the vicinity, it will, according to the research, yield you significant positive results. If you wait for the day that all the clothes are in the hamper the research would have you believe you will get to that day a lot faster if you acknowledge the steps along the way.

To be truthful, I don't know any specific research about the laundry hamper in the room since I made that up. That was my example of finding a quick easy way to acknowledge her successive approximation. Hopefully by acknowledging her improvement it motivates her to continue to improve. I know it is lame, but truthfully, giving positive attention to those efforts that approximate the desired behavior does significantly improve your odds of helping her meet the goal.

At some point in most every parent's life they think their child lied to them. Some parents choose to say nothing. Others want to talk about it.

Certainly I am in the "let's talk about it" camp, but I know parents differ on how best to respond to a lie. Rather than debate the issue, I will just share with you a way to approach the issue if you so choose.

I might say, "I need to talk about my concern that I think you may have lied to me. I don't know if you did and if you did I am not sure why you did. I just know it seems to me like you lied and that feels really bad to me. I would hope that whatever was going on with you, you would be able to speak with me about it.

"If you didn't lie I apologize and I know it probably hurts you to think that I believe you might have lied. I would totally get that. Yet if you did lie to me I would hope sometime that you would feel comfortable enough to tell me the truth. Either way I love you. I just feel bad about feeling bad."

I would like to think that I would say some version of that. I am sure others can find their own ways and point out things that I might well have wished I had said. I don't think you get to do these things perfectly. You just model the desire to be in loving truth with your child. She will do with it what she will.

If I shared my thoughts/feelings with my child and she basically just listened and then got restless and I could sense she had enough I might say, "I know this is uncomfortable to talk about, yet I am glad I shared this with you. I don't like feelings things are not straightforward between us. Let's drop it for now, unless you have something you want to share with me." Then I would let it go.

I mentioned earlier that sometimes honesty can be a weapon. There are many truths we think/feel which if shared we can pretty well guess would be quite hurtful to the other person.

Some of those truths need to be aired. Others can be left to oneself.

It is not always easy to determine if you are just being honest or if you are "sharing your truth" just to hurt the other person. While you might consider it lying to withhold the truth, you might also want to consider what is prompting your truth-sharing.

I am an advocate of being open and honest with those closest to you. I am also an advocate of self-reflection and checking out one's motives. I value getting as much clarity as possible about what is going on with me before I decide to tell someone something that I imagine will hurt them.

Of course things can get blurted out in the moment that have unforeseen reactions. Sure we have all blurted out hurtful comments that we thought we had tucked away. And we all have said something that we didn't intend to be hurtful and seen the other person get upset. We have said something that just slipped out and we wished we hadn't said it the moment it passed our lips.

Those things happen and while some self and impulse control might help you, those are not the kind of truths I am focusing on here. I am talking about something you think/feel about your partner or child that you have thought about sharing but you suspect would cause significant hurt. You have also hopefully thought about whether it really is necessary for this person to know this. Will sharing what you think/feel help them out?

If it can't pass the "I think it will be benefit them to know this" bar, it is better left unsaid.

You need to have a check-in with yourself about why you want to share something and if there is any part of you that is sharing it to hurt that person. If there is even a kernel of truth to your desire to hurt the other person, find a more direct way to deal with what is bothering you rather than throwing emotional darts. Those barbed truths are weapons and best checked at the door.

Here is a word I would like you to check at the door. It is a very potent word and while it may have done some good now and then it has caused a lot more broken spirits.

Disappointment.

As in: "You have been a disappointment to me" or "You disappoint me" or "I am disappointed in you."

I would like to take those phrases out of your vocabulary. Here's why. Children want to please parents. When your child does something displeasing to you, you might think it would motivate her if you told her you were disappointed. It does motivate some people some of the time. It may have motivated you when your parents said it. But it does other things as well.

But David, you say, sharing my disappointment is just me speaking my truth and not lying to my child about how I feel. I get that, yet saying you are disappointed in your child puts a focus on pleasing you and how important that is to you. While something may be personally important to you, it is not something you need to put on your child's shoulders. You can place a high degree of assurance on the fact that she knows when you are pleased with her and when you are not. You don't need to say a thing.

You want to build her self-esteem by having her do those things that are important to her. You don't want to overly reinforce the pleasing of others. Even if it is you.

Sure, what others think is important and what your parents think is often most important to a child. But, ultimately when she moves out of the house, she needs to build a life that pleases her. As she goes through her teen years her self-satisfaction needs to be more important than yours. While I always want my child to have an interest in pleasing me, I want her to know that what pleases me most is that she is able to build a life that pleases her.

If your child lied to you and you want to tell her that you are disappointed, not a lot of people are going to argue with that. I probably wouldn't either as your disappointment is your truth.

Yet, those words of disappointment have a long shelf-life. You might even be able to remember the things your mother and father were disappointed in about you. You might also be able to see how their disappointment shaped your life. Parental disappointment lingers in the psyche.

Rather than say, "I am disappointed in you," why not say, "Next time I hope you would..." and then fill in the desired behavior. Put the emphasis on the desired behavior, not the undesired one.

Chapter 11: Friends and Social Life

For the most part, the calls I get from parents of teenagers fall into four categories:

- Drugs/alcohol

- Stress

- Concerns that their child is having too much of social life

- Concerns that their child is not having enough of a social life

This chapter is mostly about friends and social life.

Your child will feel stress about many of the things you stress out about—relationships, school (read: work), his body, health, plans, and whatever else comes along. Of course, you probably don't have to worry about getting into college and taking the SATs or ACTS. But you have your annual review, your boss, your partner's opinions, and your worry about your child's test scores and his getting into college.

Your child may handle stress in a similar or dissimilar fashion as you. You may know when he is a little stressed and you may not know. You probably know when he is very stressed. But some teenagers try to hide the degree of their stress from their parents.

He may want your help and he may not. He may ask for your help and reject it. He may reject your help and be a little comforted when you provide it. You never fully know how your actions are received.

If you see him looking stressed and ask how he is doing he may share some of what is going on or he may say "fine" and try to move along. I usually push back a little and say, "Really? What's going on?" If he doesn't want to get into it, I let it go. If he is stressed and it continues, I would hope that eventually he would tell me something. And, I would probably ask again in a few days anyway. I can be a nudge sometimes.

You can let him know you are happy to speak with him any time and hope that when needs to he will approach you. Often, aside from hearing what your child says and commiserating with him there is often not a lot you can do. But don't minimize the value of your listening, caring, empathizing, and letting him know you are there for him.

I remember one time my teenage daughter came home from school and was very upset at one of her teachers. She thought the teacher had treated her unfairly. I did my best to commiserate with her and then I told her I would be happy to go down to the school and beat the teacher up.

She kind of laughed at that as I hope you are now doing; she knows I would never go do that. But the offer that I would do that and wanted to avenge her wrongs I hope made her feel I was on her side and had her back. I also asked if there was anything she wanted me to do and she said not to do anything. So I honored that. I was tempted to call the teacher, but I knew that was not what she wanted. But that doesn't mean I didn't think about calling for some time.

I had a mother of a 9th grader call me up and tell me she he was worried about her son. He was doing fine academically, but he didn't seem to have any real friends. He didn't go out on weekends with anyone and while he wasn't depressed he knew he would feel better if he had some friends.

Could I help him out? I told her I would try.

As a counselor at a school I can talk with faculty and ask them to do some matchmaking. Almost all classes at times break into small groups and partner up for activities. Often I ask the teachers to see what they can do about putting a student in groups where he might have a better chance of making a friend without the student ever knowing.

The magic in the teacher matchmaking is the child never knows it happened. I have to tell you that I have seen this backdoor approach to friend-making work many times. Proximity breeds familiarity, which often results in friendship. If you happen to be a parent with lack of friends concerns contact your school counselor and see what they can do.

I should also mention that most times when parents call me they ask me not to let their child know they called. Which means bringing their child into my office for a chat is challenging. Which is why I tend to work a lot with the teachers and the parents as well as the students.

A lot of times children don't have the social skills to build friendships and learning by trial and error often deters them from keeping on trying. It doesn't take too many rejections to make you wary.

Parents sometimes find themselves in the position of coaching their child on how to make friends. These can be uncomfortable discussions as your child has to expose an area where he does not feel good enough and listen to you tell him what to do to feel better. Feelings can be very easily hurt and no matter how carefully you proceed it is hard for your child to walk away from these discussions feeling less stressed. At best maybe you gave him an idea about how to approach someone. At worst you further undermined his confidence and aggravated his stress level.

Ah, what is a parent to do?

You model interacting.

You are out with him in public and you interact with a salesperson, waiter, or fellow sufferer in the checkout line where you are all waiting. You do your friendly best to throw out a semi-innocuous question, which might elicit a response. Or you are at the dinner table and you say something provocative to get a conversation going. And you continue to endeavor to do your best to have engaging conversations with him just like you would want him to have with the people he meets.

Children usually don't ask each other, "How was your day?" They often begin their conversations in the middle. For example, "The Lakers totally blew it," is a familiar opening line in Los Angeles.

I also suggest to parents that instead of starting a conversation with their child with a question they start with a statement. "You wouldn't believe what my boss made me do today," might get you more of a response than "Did you do your homework?" Model for your child the art of the inviting statement/question. He might be able to learn how to lure someone into a conversation.

But...

You at your communication modeling best are probably not going to be able to upgrade your child's social life. This is something they mostly have to do on their own. Usually with some fumbling help from someone else. Almost all children in a school end up connecting with someone. Maybe they only talk briefly during the day and never connect after school but that may not be too different from some of the people you interact with in life.

Parents hear their child say they have no friends and hated school and didn't talk to anyone. That may be true, but more than likely there are some exaggerations there. Parents get secondhand information about their child's life at school and don't really have a clear sense of what their child's day is like at school. Which is why it can help to talk to someone at the school.

Having observed high school students for over 15 years I can tell you that it is very rare for someone to not interact with at least some of his peers outside a classroom. It may not be for long and he may walk around campus alone much of the time, but most children find someone with whom they can connect on some level. We all know it is rare to find someone who you connect with on many levels, so finding someone who at least share something in common with is a good enough start.

The tricky part is getting your child to reach out.

If he happens to be an extrovert it is easier for him to initiate a conversation because he is more naturally drawn to want to engage with others. Whatever wounds and hesitancies hold him back, his nature often overcomes his fear and he reaches out. A little more cautiously.

If he keeps reaching out and getting rejected it is time for professional help. There may be things he is doing either consciously or unconsciously that are making it too difficult for people to want to be with him. There is usually some self-defeating activity that can be brought to light and options found for more positively managing the issues at play.

Since a good portion of the population are introverts, who by nature are not very comfortable initiating connections, many children will prefer to be approached than to approach. They are more comfortable when approached, but still reluctant to share much.

"How do I get my introverted child to reach out?" That is a question I am asked a lot. The answer is simple—you don't. You can try some of the things I suggest, but even those are only going to make a marginal difference. Your child will inch his way forward and ultimately he will find people with whom he can connect. It is just harder for an introvert to meet an introvert than an extrovert to meet anyone. Which also means there could very well be an extroverted kid who will reach out to your child. You never know. An introvert and an extrovert may have different communication styles but similar interests.

Parents of high school students often suffer a lot when their child does not have much or any social life. They know their child is not happy with the situation and then can't think of any new way to make things better. These parents take some refuge in the awareness that when their child leaves home they won't need to witness the isolation as much and often that child without the company of his parents does manage to reach out and form some connections. In the meantime they hurt for their child's hurt.

Even though many children, like a lot of adults, are happiest alone, their parents think they would be happier if there was more balance. They want their child to be invited to an occasional party or a movie or anywhere. When there is an absence of other children reaching out to your child it is painful. When you see how challenging it is for your child to reach out the disappointment intensifies. That's usually when my phone rings.

Boys especially have a hard time asking another guy if they want to hang out or go to a movie. It just feels awkward. It flows a lot smoother when there is a group of kids and they sort of organically stumble into making plans. When your child is not in that group, making plans with another child requires reaching out and opening himself up for rejection. Some weekends it is easier to stay home.

One way to help your child develop social skills is to get him to see a therapist who also runs groups for children his age. There are groups that teach social skills as well as groups that are educational and therapeutic. Unfortunately, there are not a lot of therapists who do groups. If you can find one, and you like the therapist, then consider signing up your child. Your school counselor may be able to help you find someone, but sadly there are not a lot of therapists who offer this service. You might check your local university as they do sometimes offer these services to the community out of their Counseling Center.

Your child won't want to go, but if he actually does learn some social skills he will quickly see that the group is helping him. If it isn't, get him out.

You could also consider individual therapy to help build his confidence and interpersonal skills. I think that is a viable path. Often people start in individual and then move on to group or do both.

With any therapy or therapist you want to be diligent about picking the therapist. I don't have the highest opinion of most of the people in the field so don't be reluctant to shop around until you find someone you believe has the warmth, knowledge, and ability to help your child.

The other major group of calls I get concerns parents who think their child may be partying too much and not spending enough time focused on his schoolwork. I don't usually get these calls until grades go home for the first time or their child gets in some kind of trouble. Fear often is the motivator to get parents to call me.

Every parent has their own agenda for how well they would like their child to do in school and how much of his life should be spent socializing, going to parties, playing games or interacting online or engulfed in YouTube and Netflix.

My advice to these parents will not surprise you. I tell them to reinforce the behaviors they want by saying something positive when they see the slightest glimpse of them happening. I would dwell less on speaking to him about the things he is doing that you don't like and more time spent talking about the things you do like. Not that you can't frown and clamp down on some of his activities. Just try to keep the frown to smile ratio in check.

Social connections mean a lot to students and they invest much of their time in interacting with their peers. You don't really want to take this source of pleasure away from your child, yet if you feel it is undermining his ability to attend to his studies and other activities you may need to do something.

Right now I want to focus more on your concern about the amount of time your child is devoting to social activities.

Natural consequences can often be a parent's best friend. If you child does something too much he will pay for it one way or the other without you doing anything. Yet, parents don't always have patience and tolerance for those consequences to take hold. They also don't want their child to have to deal with some of those consequences if they can help it. Most parents I know don't want their child to receive a poor grade that could affect his college choices. Or they don't want their child to drink too much and get into some trouble that will cause undue hardship. A little hardship along the lines of throwing up in the bathroom is fine; too much hardship is not so fine.

Parents don't want their child to suffer harsh consequences. They try to instill values and behaviors that will reduce their child's risks. As parents see their influence wane they usually lecture, discipline and worry more.

I don't think you are going to make much headway repeating your same concerns over and over with your child. I think you need to consider getting help from the school, maybe a therapist, and by approaching matters differently.

My advice is to let him be who he is in the social interactive domain of his life. It is different than when you were a child and the world is now a place of discovery and interaction that you never experienced. Let your child explore this territory. It very well may serve him in ways you will never know.

Being online in one way or the other is shaping this generation in ways we have yet to fully understand. Like most things it will have elements of the good, the bad, and the ugly. I have often found the child that has few or no friends at school has a wealth of people he connects with online.

Certainly you need the recurring lecture about online safety especially when your child is a preteen. I am sure all schools are teaching online safety but that doesn't mean some home reminders are not necessary now and then. As your teenager goes into high school and starts to actively build his resume for college he needs to know those online posts never really go away and more and more colleges are doing searches on their applicants. I just tell the students to consider all their posts to be part of their admission packet.

However your child chooses to invest his "free" time is really up to him. Most likely you will think his free time ought to be spent focusing on more productive activities, but that too is a losing battle. You can expose him to new things, provide opportunities for exploration and let him know there is more to the world then the part he is focusing on, but chastising him is not an effective approach.

What he chooses to focus on is where he feels most comfortable. You don't want to take too much of that comfort away. Rather than clamp down, think about opening up. Open up other avenues for him. He won't take all those opportunities. You don't. But he will explore some. Perhaps not now, but if the seed you plant is viable it may take root later.

Whether your child has a small or large social life you most likely would enjoy spending some time with them that was more about enjoyment and less about oversight. I just wrote a letter to the parents at the school where I work about summer vacation. I acknowledged that those lazy never-ending days of summer of our youth no longer exist for our children to the same extent. Now, like the athlete that stays in shape in the off-season so too do many students now attend to their schooling year round. Summer school, which used to be exclusively for those who did not do well in certain classes, still functions in the same way, yet now there are courses at colleges that promise a college course on your transcript and a bit of the college experience. Summers are full of community service activities and resume-building.

I encouraged parents to remember the occasional joys of summer vacation and make sure their child got some of that. The non-scheduled days. The "what should I do?" days. The "hang out with friends" days. The "lose yourself in your iPad, cell phone, or another technological instrument of the moment" days. The "do something crafty or creative" days. The "I am bored" days. And, hopefully, the "family trip" days.

Even if you can't do family trip days you can do family time together activities. Something that might actually have the word "fun" attached to it. Of course what is fun for you may cause a less than welcome a response from him. But don't let that stop you. The goal is to spend time together. Some things are more fun than others, but the idea is to do something out of the ordinary where you all get to discover new things.

Doing things together as a family is a way to open vistas for everyone. Teenagers sometimes moan about doing things with their family; they would often prefer to be with their friends. Don't let that stop you from planning activities together. Just don't overbook your child's life and his need for unstructured time. Extended family vacations or time together is usually too long for him.

Most of the students where I work have much less free time than their parents did. They have activities they do before and after school. They have sports and theater. They are on club teams, taking lessons, getting tutored, and otherwise booked up. According to Denise Pope the average middle school student spends 6.9 hours Monday through Friday on extracurricular activities. In high school that bumps up to 10.5. Plus after a day at school and possible after school activities they have to come home, relax, eat, touch base with their friends, do homework, and get to bed. Which is why most of them don't get a full night's sleep.

Almost a third of high school students study 3.5 hours a night. I am pretty sure when you were in high school that percentage was much lower. Students driven to do well often pay a high price in terms of their downtime. They don't have as much open space, play time, and just general "do nothing" time. It's no wonder with that work load that the pressures that drive a third of the student body have a ripple effect and create an ethos that is not best for all.

There is a lot for them to do in a day. A lot they are supposed to do well. A lot that will foretell what college they will be able to attend. The pressure is on.

Your job is not to add to that pressure. You need to provide the love, support, guidance, and model. You can't make your teenager do what he doesn't want to do. Well, you can. You can threaten him, entice him, or otherwise try to motivate him. But the trick of getting him to do what you want him to do is to see if you can't help him find within himself his own desire to do those things. If the things you want have no connection to what he considers important, your wishes will die on the vine.

If you can get your child to find the joy in learning and accomplishing goals, he will want to learn more and do more. The best way to help him find that motivation is for you to give him some positive attention when he is doing the things you want and to occasionally ask him how he feels about doing the things he is doing. When he gets a better grade from studying it incentivizes him to want to continue. When he studies hard and gets a poor grade it de-incentivizes him Which is when you need to step in and give him an extra dose of appreciation for working hard, and a bit of that old "If at first you don't succeed, try try again" speech. Then say, "Ugh. I'm sorry it didn't work out well. Hang in there."

Chapter 12: Everything Parenting

Parenting is a lifetime occupation. Once you get the job you keep the job. Even in those horrible instances where parents lose their child, that does not stop them from having an ongoing relationship with their child. Just because someone dies does not mean your relationship with them ends. It just moves into a different realm.

As I have mentioned, parenting is a sacred trust. Not everyone gets to be a parent.

Every parent knows that what you think about parenting when you don't have children is significantly different than what you experience when you are a parent. Others can talk, think, and write about it, but living it is where the magic rests.

Your life as a parent has transformed you in ways you didn't fully grasp. You no longer are the person you were before you had children. You are forever changed.

With that transformation comes a covenant with life.

Not every parent takes on the full vow of parenthood and in truth we all make our own vows. Most of which are never fully spoken or fully realized until time reveals them or someone asks.

You may not have fully lived up to the vows you made, just as many people do not fully live up to the vows they make when they marry. We mostly all start with the best of intentions and then do our best to live up to them.

What you will and won't do for your child differs from parent to parent. Most parents will do things and feel things for their children that they don't feel and do quite the same with anyone else. There are bonds that connect family members that don't exist with others. Blood is thicker than water and the blood of a parent that flows to their child often runs thickest of all.

There are people who believe you should love yourself above all others.

There are people who believe you should love your spouse above all others.

There are people who believe you should love your children above all others.

There are people who believe you should love none above others.

There are people who believe you should love your God, your country, your sports team, and your pet above all others.

We can all believe what we want. We are fortunate to live in a country that promotes individual beliefs. Yet what we believe and what we do day to day don't always walk arm-in-arm.

Whatever the priorities of your love and however much you fulfill them, if you have a child there is someone on this earth who is a direct descendent of you and your forbearers. There is someone on this earth who is of you and who will carry forth your heritage.

For some, that holds a level of pride and responsibility. For others it doesn't mean that much.

If being connected to your forbearers does happen to mean something to you and you want to honor the lineage of your family, be sure to make efforts to convey those values, stories, and heirlooms that carry meaning for you. Whether you are sharing a funny anecdote about a grandparent or aunt or uncle, you are sharing your family history and giving your child a sense of what it has been to be a member of this clan. I encourage you to have those talks with your child.

I remember a day when my mother walked me around her house and told me what she wanted me to know about each item of importance to her and each item she wanted me to save. I didn't like that conversation because I knew it meant one day my mother would die and I would inherit her life. Yet it was a meaningful conversation to us both and we repeated it in various forms over the years. Like some other emotionally challenging discussions, those conversations made us cry, laugh, and grow closer together. I am grateful for them and thankful she took the time to let me know what was important to her.

Have I respected everything she told me in a way she could respect? Probably some things more than others. But like many parents, I have found myself talking to my child and heard my mother's voice.

Most people don't want to talk about their own death, let alone to their child. While I do think it is something you need to do, I also know that for most people there is a lot of procrastination. While there may be no apparent rush there also is some rush because you know you never know. I think it is easier to share what is meaningful to you in your life with your child in casual conversations throughout your lifetime. Until you feel brave enough and think your child is ready, you can save telling him, "Let's sit down and talk about my will and the things I think you ought to know on the occasion of my demise. Whenever it is."

Just don't wait too long.

I remember being at a Jackson Browne concert with my teenage daughter and when he played For a Dancer I told her I wanted that song played at my funeral. She looked at me with a pained expression and later told me it was weird and she could never hear that song again without thinking about what I said. That was okay with me. Not great, but a step in the process of shifting generations. I also knew that when I died she would play that song and we would be connected in that moment. Now, I hear that song and cry and think of the love I share with her. Those tears mean a lot to me.

While that was a direct "when I die" comment, there are many more stories you can share that have nothing to do with death but everything to do with what have been hallmarks of your family's history.

If you want to get an early start on this I recommend connecting your child with the articles around your home in storytelling ways. Everything you have has a story. Some worth telling. Some not. Some forgotten.

While you still can remember the stories, sprinkle anecdotes into your conversations until you hear, "Not again. I have heard that story too many times." Then you know your work has been done.

You are the historian of your family. Share your oral history. If you are inclined you can write up the stories or go around to the pictures you have in the house and stick a note on the back that explains it.

When you are home together and something organically comes up, you can weave in the "I would like you to keep this item" comments. Your child will learn what has meaning to you and when the time comes he will be inclined to keep the ones with the most meaning.

Not always, but mostly.

Just like you have done.

Or haven't.

Just as you will always be your child's parent, so too will he always be his parent's child.

If you live long enough you may become your child's child and he his parent's parent. It doesn't hurt to keep that in mind. You may want/need him sometime to be there for you in ways you were there for him. Chances are he will interact with you with the same level of TLC you have given him.

As a parent you can only do your best and know it isn't perfect.

You may wish you had done better.

You may wish that your relationship with your child was better and you may wish you could have done some things differently.

Just as your relationship with your parents was not perfect, neither is yours with your child nor his with you. It is a relationship after all.

Until the moment you die, you have the ongoing ability to continue to do your best and let your child know you want things to be as good as they can be between you, and as good as they can be for him in his life away from you.

Love your children as best you can.

Love you as best you can.

Love your life as best you can and do your best to be gentle to yourself and others as we all learn how to live on this earth in peace and harmony.

Conclusion

Again, I thank you for reading this essential guide for parents of teenage boys. As parents, I trust your journey will be a loving one and that the teenage son who challenges you today will become a man who brings the world the sterling values it most ardently craves.

If you enjoyed this book and you thought it will benefit you, I would appreciate it if you would leave me an Amazon review by clicking here.

All the best in your journey!

Printed in Great Britain
by Amazon